The Extraord
the Castle

Knaresborough, 1865

JT Glew

Acknowledgements

I'd like to thank the following people and organisations for their part in making this book happen:

- Knaresborough Museum Association, for prioritising the story and letting me run with it
- The British Newspaper Archive
- The National Library of Scotland, for permission to reproduce the maps
- Ian Garbutt, for permission to reproduce images from Isabel Garbutt's postcard collection
- Tony Newbould, for permission to reproduce his father's photographs
- Ruth Bulmer from KMA, for reading through the drafts
- Other researchers who shared their insights - Howard Johnson, Derrick McRobert, Gail Townrow, Michael and Ann Brett

Contents

Foreword

In the spring of 2022, having spent several years thoroughly enjoying researching my own family's history, I signed up as a research volunteer for Knaresborough Museum Association, then in the planning stages of an exciting project to open a community-run Knaresborough Town Museum.

I was asked to see what I could find out about an all but forgotten event in the town's history – a so-called riot which took place in 1865 for which eleven men were sent to prison for asserting what they perceived to be the common right of access to the ground and footpaths in the Castle Yard. The townsfolk's response following the release of the Eleven from prison was something completely unprecedented.

The events of 1865 and 1866 were brought to the town's attention some ten years ago by Howard Johnson, the great-grandson of one of the rioters, who had already done a considerable amount of work to uncover the story. Working with the Knaresborough Civic Society, Howard was instrumental in the provision of a blue plaque, which now hangs on a wall in the Castle Yard, commemorating the event. He very kindly gave me some excellent starting points and contacts.

Some research had also been carried out by Derrick McRobert, who had discovered the story whilst restoring the bell-ringing archives for St John's church and had become fascinated by the achievements of rioter Joseph Harper Kearton.

It turned out that the events, and especially the extraordinary response of the town of Knaresborough, had captured the imagination of the newspapers of the time in a big way, and as the story started to unfold in the coverage of the initial hearing, the trial itself, and subsequent developments, it was clear that it deserved a full-length book.

I have tried to tell the story as faithfully as possible to the way it emerged in the newspapers.

The second half of the book focuses on the life stories of the key players.

Introduction

Mr Justice Shee:

"You have all been found guilty of this riot and unfortunately it appears that you took the law into your own hands in a country where everybody has the right to legal redress of his grievance [...]

Attending as I do to the recommendations of this jury [for the sentence to be tempered with mercy], I do not feel myself at liberty to pass a less severe sentence than the one I now pass which is that you each be imprisoned with hard labour for three months"

The Knaresborough Rioters, *Leeds Intelligencer,* the 7th of April 1866

On Friday the 6th of April 1866, eleven honest and true men of Knaresborough were sentenced to three months imprisonment with hard labour in Wakefield Gaol. The overwhelming reaction of the inhabitants of Knaresborough was a response the like of which the town had never before witnessed. It is a story which deserves to be told.

The men in question were: **John Winterburn**, aged 17, a mechanic at the linen mill; **Joseph Kearton** aged 18, a music teacher; **Peter Robinson** aged 19, an iron moulder; **George Renton** aged 20, a surveyor's assistant; **Thomas Barker**, aged 22, a labourer; **William Ranson**, aged 48, a shoemaker; **James Fletcher**, aged 52, a labourer; **Thomas Mawson**, aged 54, a joiner; **William Procter**, aged 56, a linen bleacher; **Henry Dixon**, aged 61, a furniture broker; and **Thomas Johnson**, aged 62, a mason's labourer.

3

Part I: The story

Monday the 2nd of October, 1865

On the night of the 2nd of October, John Simpson was at home with his family at their London residence in Gloucester Place, Marylebone. He had left Castle Lodge unoccupied save for Elizabeth Osborne, the Cook, and housemaid Lissie Bell[1]. His gardener, Burgess, would be over in the morning with the man Smith, there being much to do in the grounds at this time of year. If he were aware of the next day's public meeting it was not enough to send him running back up to Yorkshire.

He had always had a soft spot for Castle Lodge, which had belonged to him since he was a young man. Back in 1825, as a newly qualified physician, working in Bradford on the insistence of his uncle[2], he had often sought reasons to return to the town where he was born. When people visited, he would take them to see the extraordinary views over the river Nidd from the house in Knaresborough and from his friend Richard Gallon's house further down the street. He would sometimes just stand watching the rooks circling around the oak trees on the far side of the river.

The young Dr Simpson of 1825 had been no different from any young man of privilege of his era. Although he had enough

---

[1] These were the servants at Castle Lodge in the 1861 Census, four years earlier, when Dr Simpson's daughters Agnes and Rosa were staying there. We are told in a report of the Castle Yard Trial that as well as the gardener, Burgess, there were two female servants on the premises on the day of the riot, but they are not named.
[2] His benefactor, Dr John Simpson of Malton, from whom he later inherited.

money for a comfortable life, it was not enough to give up working. He found the cases he treated as a physician somewhat interesting. He enjoyed evenings of music and dancing in the company of young ladies, musing what it would be like to one day take a wife. He spent time with his friends discussing current affairs and playing whist and chess. He and some colleagues planned to start a Bradford newspaper. He read much but suffered from an underlying boredom.

At the time, Bradford was not a place he would have chosen to be. He was not enamoured of the Bradford manufacturing classes, writing with all the arrogance of youth *"The lower order of people are little removed above brute creation, being the rudest and most vulgar people under the sun"*[3].

His dream, often expressed, had been to find a place, maybe in Harrogate,

> *"[...] a few acres of land on which I should build a neat small house with suitable out offices and surround them with proper shrubs and plantations. If there was only a small supply of water and two or three acres of ground, I could make the most beautiful place of it. I have a small estate situated between Harrogate and Knaresborough*[4]*, which I would take into my own management and indulge my taste for rural pursuits at the same time that I might improve the land and increase the income derived from it. I frequently think of removing there [Harrogate] as I'm certain I should feel much happier. Neither do I suppose I should be a*

---

[3] The Journal of Dr John Simpson of Bradford 1825
[4] The small estate seems to be 18 acres of land between Knaresborough and Starbeck which he mentions in elsewhere in the same Journal as being let to a farmer for £35

loser in points of professional remuneration.
There is only one circumstance present
prevents me and that is the fear of offending
my uncle - if it were not for that I should not
remain one more week in Bradford. "

The Journal of Dr John Simpson of Bradford 1825

Of course, by the time he was in a position to leave Bradford, he had inherited his uncle's estate and no longer needed to think about "points of professional remuneration".

In 1825, it had not occurred to him that Castle Lodge might one day become the country retreat of his dreams.

Within a few years he had married Elizabeth, started a family, and eventually settled at Cayton Hall. In Cayton, John Simpson was finally living the life for which he had yearned, a grand home in the country with nine servants, freeing him up to follow his rural pursuits.

Meanwhile his house in Knaresborough stood empty[5]. In the 1840s he had let some of the land around it in three plots as gardens[6].

It wasn't until the family had moved to their London home (21 Gloucester Place in Portland Square, Marylebone), leaving Cayton in the hands of friend and magistrate Thomas Clifton Wilkinson and his family, that John Simpson had begun to show an interest in his country residence at Castle Lodge again.

Needing a pied-a-terre from which to carry out his duties as West Riding magistrate, and somewhere to which he could escape

---

[5] In 1851, one of the houses in "Dr Simpson's Yard" - presumably Castle Lodge - was uninhabited on the day of the census. The house next door – Castle Cliff – was occupied by Edwin Smith, clerk to the Improvement Commissioners, and his family, in that census and for more than 30 years afterwards
[6] Tithe Apportionment, 1845

from city life, he had started spending more time there. He took back the land that had been let as gardens and additional land going down towards the river which he rented from Sir Charles Slingsby and started developing the pleasure grounds of his dreams.

In 1855, he enquired of the Duke of Devonshire whether the Duchy would allow him to lease about a rood[7] of land adjoining his existing property so that he could fill in the Castle ditch which had for a long time been full of rubbish and foul-smelling. The Duchy gave him the lease at the rate of £1 per annum and he set about planting fine shrubs and trees. John Simpson was very pleased with the result. As far as he was concerned, his developments beautified and improved the area immeasurably to the admiration of all who saw it.

Without any thought to the traditions and rights of the people of the town, who had for centuries used that patch of ground for recreation, he then made the mistake of enclosing it with fences and a locked gate to keep the people out. That was the start of a run of disputes with the people of Knaresborough that had resulted in him having to move his boundaries several times.

It was an annoyance. John Simpson was by now 72 years old, no longer a young man, and age had done nothing to improve his tolerance. All he desired was peace and quiet and to enjoy the beautiful environment he had created around himself. Recently it seemed every time he had taken a walk in his grounds, his enjoyment was spoiled by the noise and laughter coming from the children at the National School next door. He wrote to the trustees complaining that the school should not allow *"shouts, screams and other noises"*[8] and threatening legal action.

---

[7] Equivalent to ¼ acre
[8] 'Dr Simpson and the Vicar of Knaresborough - castle yard riots' *Richmond and Ripon Chronicle Saturday, 4th November 1865*

He thought that his troubles were caused by a small group of malevolent individuals, and that while this was irksome, he need not pay too much attention to it. On the night of the 2nd of October, he slept soundly in his bed.

Knaresborough Castle, Pre-1905. Reproduced with permission, from the postcard collection of Isabel Garbutt.

Tuesday the 3rd of October, 1865...

Dr Simpson had seriously misjudged feeling in the town. His popularity amongst the townspeople was already not running high. They objected strongly to his high-handed attitude towards their right of access across the land he had enclosed, barring them from using their traditional place of recreation and blocking the footpath down to Castle Mill where many of them worked. But the idea of complaining about children's laughter caused widespread outrage and consternation amongst all sectors of the community.

With potential trouble brewing, the Town Constable called a public meeting to be held at the courthouse on Tuesday afternoon. Its main purpose was to discuss what should be done about Dr Simpson's complaint, and to open a public subscription to pay for a defence counsel for the trustees of the National School should Simpson carry out his threat of legal action.

On the afternoon of Tuesday the 3rd of October, anybody who could free themselves from the responsibilities of daily life for a couple of hours made their way to the courthouse to the public meeting.

The meeting was presided over by the Vicar. Amongst the crowd was Gilbert Archy, sergeant of police. Archy had been a policeman in Knaresborough for eight years and was well-known in the town. The swarthy dark-haired Irishman had defused many an awkward situation over the years. The meeting was well run and he maintained a discreet background presence. The discussions inevitably strayed towards previous incidents involving Dr Simpson's encroachment on to the Castle Yard. Archy kept a close eye on **the man in the shadows at the back of the room** who had caused trouble in the past and young

George Renton who had been too young to take part in previous incidents but seemed to have a lot to say for himself today.

The meeting came to a close about four o'clock and people spilled out into the Castle Yard. They were stood around in small groups talking amongst themselves about what had just passed. Archy was aware that George Renton was gathering a small crowd of people around him. He followed as the crowd led by Renton moved towards the gates to Dr Simpson's grounds. He saw Renton try the gates and heard the gardener, Burgess, say "They are not fastened".

Superintendent Robert Seymour Ormsby was watching from the window of his office. Like his sergeant, Gilbert Archy, Robert Ormsby was an Irishman from Sligo. He had signed up at the age of twenty-eight for the new West Riding Constabulary in its inaugural year following the Borough and County Constabulary Act of 1856. He was an experienced leader of men having been a Captain of the Sligo Rifles militia. Within a couple of months, he was promoted first to Inspector and then Superintendent. Some of his force still referred to him as "Captain" Ormsby.

Robert Ormsby had been Superintendent of Police during previous incidents involving Dr Simpson's enclosures and was prepared for the possibility of something kicking off after the meeting. He had already decided to keep the police response as low key as possible. He only had a small number of men at his disposal. Moreover, he was mindful that the Court of the Queen's Bench had previously ruled that the people DID have right of access to the Castle Yard ground.

He wandered across the Castle Yard to have a word with his sergeant and to see for himself what was happening. The two of them walked together back to the office and briefed the handful of officers who were available. As far as was possible, the approach was to be one of "friendly advice".

The gardener, William Burgess

Burgess had not gone to the meeting at the courthouse. There was a lot of work to do in Dr Simpson's pleasure grounds at the start of autumn to keep the gardens looking good. He was alert to the possibility that there might be trouble following the meeting. He personally thought it was a bad error of judgement on the part of his employer to give the people another reason to rake up their grievances about the enclosure of the Duchy land. What was so bad about the sound of children playing? But he was not the man to tell him that!

He made sure the gates were unfastened – he did not want anyone breaking the locks again – he secured the gates to the private flower garden and then went on about his work.

The meeting finished about four o'clock. He saw young George Renton approaching with a crowd around him and met them at the gates near the infants' school. Renton tried the lock and Burgess told him it was not fastened, and they could come in. Renton and Henry Dixon entered the ground and were followed by others in ones and twos until the place was full of people. Somebody left and returned with a large hammer and a crowbar, and so the work of restoring the common land began.

They started with the tree guards and the trees outside of the present gates, where Dr Simpson's earlier attempts at enclosure had been. Burgess recognised Thomas Johnson and James Fletcher. The gates were flanked with iron railings and a pair of stone pillars with acorns on top. He saw Johnson move away from the trees and climb one of the stone gate pillars. His friend Henry Dixon passed the sledgehammer up to him and he proceeded to strike the stone acorn until he managed to knock it off the top of the pillar. Some other men joined him, and they broke up the ornament and railings.

At that point Burgess became aware that people were heading towards another part of the garden, and he rushed off to secure the doors to the vinery just to be on the safe side. To be fair, the men seemed to be confining themselves to that part of the grounds over which they thought the public had rights and were not attempting to approach the house or the private flower gardens. He did not see anyone in that area. On his way back by a different path, he noticed John Winterburn chopping down a beech tree. William Procter was cutting a bar at the base of the railings. William Ranson was standing nearby with a saw under his arm.

The gardener climbed up the steps toward the summerhouse – a hut with a low brick wall and a ling-thatched roof supported by beech poles. Several men were rocking it, intending to roll it down the bank. He knew that Dr Simpson had erected the little hut at considerable expense. When he reached the summerhouse, he saw that it was on fire and realised that with its roof of heather it would quickly ignite, and he would be powerless to do anything about it. He could not get through the people to put water on it. By this time the work had been going on for about an hour. Many people were standing by watching, they came and they went, in good spirits. Nobody troubled the gardener.

Branches from the chopped down trees were being thrown on the fire. So were some of the fence panels. It continued to burn well into the night.

Against the wall that bounded the school yard, there was fragrant jasmine and a beautiful silver-leaved ivy. Burgess did try to save the ivy, but the crowd pushed him away and started attacking the vine. It was a young plant, its stem no thicker than a man's thumb. He heard someone say "cut into it" and someone else "let's get it out at any rate". Thomas Benson the whitesmith, a neighbour, came to the gardener's assistance [9]. In the brief moment of confusion when the crowd had driven Burgess back,

---

[9] In the 1861 Census, Thomas Benson was living with his wife Sarah and three daughters (5, 3 and 11 months) on Kirkgate at the entrance to Dr Simpson's Yard.

he couldn't say later whether the ivy had been cut down or ripped out.

The youth, Jack Winterburn, was near by – he remembered that – and still had the axe in his hand from chopping down the beech and a small poplar. Burgess didn't see him use it anywhere near the ivy though. Just about then, a lad from the mill - Joseph Bradley, a moulder – came to fetch Winterburn back to his place of work. He said he would come and left the axe on the ground.

Burgess later heard that a magistrate had been present whilst the disturbance was going on. He didn't see him; he did see the police constables though. He didn't ask the police to interfere. He wasn't concerned that anyone might be harmed. Some of the most respectable people of Knaresborough were there, and nobody tried to stop the proceedings.

It was midnight before the grounds were completely clear of people.

The following morning, when they went to inspect the damage, damp down the last glowing embers from the summerhouse, and take photos of the devastation[10], they discovered that twenty-nine trees had been felled with an axe and a further fifty-eight had been sawn… and that was not taking into account the shrubs. The damage was estimated at more than £322.

---

[10] The newspaper reports stated that photographs had been taken, and exhibited as evidence at the court hearing. Given that photography was a relatively new technology and still very expensive, this is an indication of how seriously the incident was taken by Dr Simpson.

The police

Superintendent Ormsby had only Gilbert Archy and four other men at his disposal that afternoon - Joseph Eastwood (Warrant No. 1297), Fleming Brooks (Warrant No. 1704), William Barret Hudson (Warrant No. 1504) and another. Had he seen the magistrate there he could have requested the assistance of special constables but in any case, he was wary of interfering too much when he understood the people to have a legitimate grievance.

He stationed two of the officers by some posts and gave them instructions not to let anyone go any further than that. He and Sergeant Archy, and the two other officers, maintained a presence in the grounds. People came and went. It was difficult to estimate numbers, but the general consensus was around 200-300 at any one time, maybe a thousand over the whole evening. By far the majority of the people there were simply onlookers, in good spirits and quietly enjoying the spectacle. He reckoned for the most part the mischief was carried out by around 25 men.

A man stood back in the shadows, watching. Like Gilbert Archy during the public meeting, Robert Ormsby knew the man and was expecting trouble, but none came.

On the other hand, he was not really surprised that, having led the crowd to the gates in the first place, young George Renton did not cause any further disturbance other than to offer his wholehearted encouragement. He knew that people in the town looked up to Renton and his grandfather, George Renton Snr. They lived at the sheriff's office. in his younger days, the old man had been Keeper of the Gaol of the Forest and Liberty of Knaresborough. He had pursued his duties with firmness and compassion – he himself had been in the debtors' prison on one occasion – and was respected by many of the prisoners whom he had steered through the system at hard times in their lives. His business as an auctioneer, surveyor and land valuer had been established for nearly forty years and its reputation well-known throughout the district. His grandson had lived with him since his mother died, and he had instilled in George Jnr. both the skills of his profession and a strong set of values.

Robert Ormsby saw George Renton sitting on a wall, handing beer to the men from a stone jug. Dixon had also gone home and fetched a pitcher of beer for the workers. The Superintendent had a quiet word with Dixon. *"You know if you get the men drunk you will be to some extent responsible for their actions"*. Dixon replied that they were working hard, and it was thirsty work, they deserved a drink.

They were about 25 or 30 yards from the summerhouse. A cry of "Fire!" was heard. Superintendent Ormsby looked over and noticed a young man run a lighted match along the heather near to the hut. He sent PC Eastwood over to enquire as to the young man's name. It was Thomas Barker. The flames took hold quickly, and he saw another lad touch a light to it. He recognised him as the teenager with the wonderful voice from the church choir – Joseph Kearton. He noted that he'd seen Kearton earlier breaking up some branches.

Meanwhile Sergeant Archy was having a word with some of the other men. He said to them *"You are great fools to do this"*. Thomas Mawson was sawing away at a wooden railing. He told the others *"If we mind our business, Archy will mind his"* and carried on working. Archy said no more to him and walked away.

The disturbance was over in two or three hours and, satisfied with what they had achieved, the crowd started to disperse.

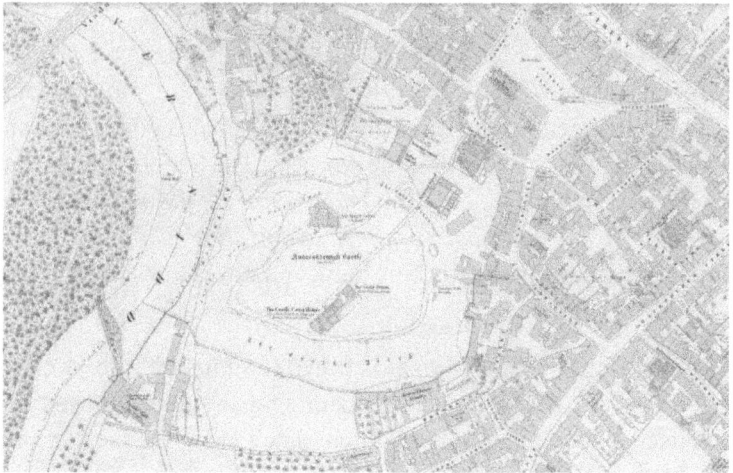

Extract from Ordnance Survey Town Plans, Knaresborough - Sheet 3, Surveyed: 1849, Published: 1851. Reproduced with the permission of the National Library of Scotland.

Bishopgate Series No. 15830, Knaresborough and Castle from the Air. Reproduced with permission, from the postcard collection of Isabel Garbutt.

Wednesday the 1st of November, 1865...

Four weeks passed and the disturbance at the Castle Yard ceased to be the only subject of conversation in the pub and in neighbours' back yards. Of the twenty-five or so people who actively participated in the demolition of Dr Simpson's encroachments, eleven were summoned by Mr Matthew Gill, solicitor's clerk, to appear at a hearing on Wednesday the 1st of November at the courthouse. The presiding magistrates were Messrs Lawson, Faviell and Brown. Dr John Simpson being well-known by every member of the Bench, several local magistrates had refused to act in the matter. Mr Middleton, barrister, appeared for the prosecution and Mr Blackburn, barrister for the defence.

Mr Middleton warned that some of the witnesses would attempt to show that their common right of access to the ground over-rode the jurisdiction of the magistrates. But even if this were true, to assemble for riotous demolition constituted an indictable offence.

Burgess, the gardener, and Superintendent Ormsby, Sergeant Gilbert Archy and police officer Joseph Eastwood gave their evidence. They all, under examination and cross-examination, identified the defendants as having been present at the scene on the day – that was not in question. They made it clear that the defendants only caused damage in the area over which everyone believed they have rights. They all said that the crowd were in good spirits and denied feeling intimidated or threatened.

At 5 o'clock there were several witnesses still to be heard. The case was adjourned until Friday.

In all sixteen of the most respected inhabitants of the town spoke in favour of the defendants and denied that the men's actions constituted a riot on this occasion. Eventually however all eleven were bound over to appear for trial at the next Leeds assizes on the charge of riot and destruction of property. Bail was set at £20[11]. A secondary charge of arson against the three youths – Kearton, Barker and Robinson – was abandoned.

The town immediately rallied round to raise funds for a defence counsel for the men, and to make sure that the wives and children of those who were married would not suffer hardship should the worst happen and they be sent to prison.

---

[11] The schedule of trials states that they were admitted for bail on Friday 3rd November. I was told this was set at £20 but have not found a source for that.

Friday the 6th of April, 1866...

A riot or not a riot?

> *"Riot is a tumultuous disturbance of the peace by three persons or more assembling together of their own authority with an intent mutually to assist one another against anyone who shall oppress them in the execution of some enterprise of a private nature, and afterwards executing the same in a violent and turbulent manner to the terror of people whether the act intended would of itself lawful or unlawful.* [12] *"*

Mr Shepherd, defence counsel for George Renton

Some five months later, on the 6th of April 1866, the "Knaresborough Eleven" appeared at the Leeds Assizes before Mr Justice Shee. For the prosecution were Mr Middleton and Mr Campbell Foster, and for the defence Mr Digby Seymour QC and Mr Blackburn, except for George Renton who was defended by Mr Shepherd. Since the case for Renton was no different from the case for the rest of them, Mr Shepherd for the most part left proceedings in the hands of Mr Seymour.

Mr Middleton opened for the prosecution by saying that if three or more people assemble together riotously and tumultuously to disturb the peace and cause damage to a church, chapel, malthouse, coach house or other similar "erection" they were

---

[12] 'The Knaresborough Riot:- question of public right' *Sheffield Daily Telegraph*, 7 April 1866

subject to penalties, regardless of whether the intention of their action was lawful or not.

During the long debate that followed, it was agreed that the public meeting held in the courthouse had been lawful; there was a question whether the summer house, which had been burnt down, constituted an "other erection" under the terms of the Act; then whether intimidation and terror had been caused, and whether the axes, saws and other tools fetched by the men could be construed as arms. It was noted that the ladies present were not afraid, that the police officers had not seen fit to intervene and that spirits were generally good. Although the men had only worked on restoring what they believed to be the common ground, and not touched anything else of Dr Simpson's, the Judge said it was not for them to decide if it were common ground or not.

The submission of a late witness statement took everyone, both prosecution and defence, by surprise. It was the testimony of Thomas Benson, the neighbour who had come to Burgess's aid. He had not been required by Mr Gill to submit a deposition at the initial hearing, and had not come forward then.

Benson claimed that while he was helping Burgess protect the silver-leaved ivy, he heard John Winterburn say, "Stand by or I'll chop thy bloody legs off!". There was a gasp of shock in the courtroom. Not one other witness had said they had seen or heard anything of a threatening nature. Burgess himself had said nothing about this.

Benson's statement changed everything. The prosecution could now claim intimidation.

The jury retired at around five o'clock, returning to the courtroom a while later to clarify a point of law around Thomas Benson's unexpected witness testimony. Mr Justice Shee said that if Winterburn's words had caused Burgess and Benson to stop doing what they could to protect Dr Simpson's property, then

20

even if it were only one person, terror and intimidation had been caused and they should pass a verdict of Guilty. There was no other evidence at all of anyone being afraid.

At around eight o'clock, the Foreman of the Jury approached the Bench and said that they had reached a verdict of Guilty, but that they were uneasy about it, and he would like to explain the jurors' reasons for doing so. Mr Justice Shee declined to hear the reasons. The Foreman asked that any sentence be tempered with mercy.

Mr Justice Shee acknowledged that the men did not do any actual violence to Burgess and did not trespass beyond that part of Dr Simpson's grounds over which they imagined those who had gone before them in Knaresborough had some rights of recreation. Nevertheless, his sentence of three months' imprisonment with hard labour left the townsfolk shocked.

The aftermath

"...five sixths of the people in Knaresborough were evidently of the opinion that the men were acting in the bona fide assertion of a public right and if they were technically guilty of a riot the sentence was excessive"

'Reception of the Knaresboro Rioters' *Richmond and Ripon Chronicle*, 30 June 1866

Within a week, the town had sent a letter to Sir George Grey, the Home Secretary, pleading for commutation of the sentence. Upwards of one thousand signatures were obtained *"including the clergy, gentry, and nearly every respectable inhabitant of the town*[13]*"*

This was unsuccessful.

Powerless to shorten or overturn the men's sentence, on the Saturday immediately after the trial several of the town's elders were talking about the dire state of affairs. Mr Howe said that something should be done to give those who had been convicted a worthy reception on their return. They arranged to meet on Monday and convene a proper committee to act upon this idea.

The committee proposed to open a fund with contributions to be from two pence to three shillings a week. The amount they collected far exceeded their expectations and instead of getting £3 a week as was anticipated they had obtained between £7 and £8. People of all social stations came forward and the sympathy was so great that instead of keeping the subscription list open for the whole 12 weeks they found they had sufficient funds in six

---

[13] 'The Knaresborough Riot' *Richmond and Ripon Chronicle*, 14 Apr 1866

weeks with enough left over to make any presentation that they liked.

They considered what they could do to show the Eleven that regardless of what the so-called justice system or anyone else thought, the town of Knaresborough was fully behind them and far from thinking poorly of them for having a conviction to their names, considered them heroes. It was agreed that some of the money raised should be used to have silver tankards made for each and every one of them and engraved with words of thanks.

George Renton's grandfather, Mr George Renton Snr, requested special dispensation from the magistrates to visit his grandson in Wakefield Gaol and relay to him the efforts that were being made on the men's behalf. This was not normal practice, but George Renton Snr's position as Sheriff's Officer and former keeper of the Gaol of the Forest and Liberty of Knaresborough undoubtedly helped his case.

In the meantime, there was the thorny question of Thomas Benson's unexpected testimony. Had he for some reason perjured himself?

Three days after the riot at Dr Simpson's, **John Snowden, the clog-maker**, had had a conversation with Thomas Benson. Snowden knew something that many others may not have known – that Benson had been a witness a few years earlier regarding the previous incident at Dr Simpson's[14]. Benson said that he had had nothing to do with it this latest time, that he had seen nothing and knew nothing much about it. John Snowden did not know that on the very evening of that conversation, Benson had been called to Mr Gill's to be examined.

Edward Myers, the publican at the Golden Anchor on the High Street, had a similar conversation with Benson only a

---

[14] At this previous incident in 1860, a James Snowden was one of the accused and Thomas Benson a witness.

couple of weeks before the trial. Benson had asked him "What do you think about this affair?" With the diplomacy of a publican, he said he did not know. Benson replied, *"I'm very glad that I had nothing to do with it this time. I know nothing about it, and I'm proud of being clear of it"*.

Myers had been in the magistrates' court at Knaresborough back in November when the men were first charged with riot. His brother-in-law was one of the accused. Benson had not been examined as a witness. Edward Myers was as surprised as everyone else at Benson's last-minute decision to come forward at the Leeds Assizes.

Just before the trial, **William Haress** had been stopped in the street by Mr Kaye, the shoemaker, with whom he was on nodding terms. He was standing in his doorway. Mr Kaye asked him if he intended going to the trial in Leeds to hear the case. He said he might. He had wondered why the shoemaker was asking him about it but couldn't remember later what he had said to him. Not much, he thought.

He had not lived in the town for long. He had come for a labouring job. He had been at Dr Simpson's grounds during the disturbance, not entirely sure what the whole thing was about.

He was a bit concerned when the man Benson had come to him three weeks ago and ORDERED him to go and see Mr Gill, the solicitor's clerk. He was most insistent. He didn't know Benson very well but had heard his unexpected evidence at the trial. William didn't know why Benson had required him to see Mr Gill. He just said it would be about the castle yard disturbances. Until he arrived at Mr Gill's he had no idea what they were going to ask him about. He answered their questions as best he could, saying that he had been near the ivy when John Winterburn was there and he thought he had heard him swear if they did not stand by, he would chop somebody's bloody legs off.

24

Tuesday the 8th of May, 1866...

The perjury of Thomas Benson

A charge of perjury against Thomas Benson of Knaresborough was inquired into on Tuesday the 8th of May in front of the Leeds magistrates. The case had been before the magistrates a few days earlier but had been adjourned so that they could produce the certificate of John Winterburn's conviction.

Mr Shaw appeared for the prosecution and Mr Middleton for the defence. Mr Shaw opened by briefly recalling the events thus far. He said that the testimony of Thomas Benson was of vital importance as, in order to claim a riot had taken place, it must be shown that people were in bodily terror. Mr Shaw found that Benson was the **only man who spoke to a threat of the kind being used.**

Moreover, Benson was not one of the witnesses bound over before the magistrates as he **had not made any deposition at all** at Knaresborough during the initial investigation.

Mr John Kirby, solicitor of Knaresborough, who had been at the trial and heard Benson's examination, and **Robert Ackrill** of Harrogate, a reporter who had been at the trial and taken down Benson's evidence in longhand, were the first to be called as witnesses and confirmed Mr Shaw's opening statements.

The certificate of Winterburn's conviction was then put in and read.

John Winterburn, having been brought up from Wakefield prison by a judge's order, took the stand. The 17-year-old remained calm and answered the questions asked of him plainly.

JW: *I am one of the persons who was indicted at the last Leeds assizes for rioting at Knaresborough and I am one of a number who went to Dr Simpson's residence on the 3rd of October to remove what we thought to be encroachments. There was a silver leaved Ivy on what we considered to be a part of the land. We went about quarter to six. I saw [Thomas] Benson there. I never spoke a word to him.*

MR SHAW: Did you say to him "Stand by or I will chop off your bloody or damned legs"?

JW: *I did not.*

MR SHAW: Did you use these words to anyone?

JW: *I did not.*

MR MIDDLETON: Is it true you had an axe in your hand?

JW: *It is. Benson took hold of me and tried to pull me away, but he could not. He turned to a man called James Hatley and said you pull him away I cannot. Hatley got hold of me and said do not be a fool, and a boy came to fetch me to my work. All I said to Hatley was "I will go". He then let me go.*

MR SHAW: Did you not chop down the silver leaved ivy before you went?

JW: *No I did not.*

MR MIDDLETON: Do you know a person of the name of William Haress?

JW: *I do not.*

Haress was brought into court, and on the question being repeated to Winterburn he said *I knew him by sight (laughter).*

MR MIDDLETON: Now Sir, did you see [Haress] close to the silver leaved Ivy when it was cut down?

JW: *No but he might have been there I suppose.*

26

JW: *He might have been. I did not hear any other violent language used. I was neither drunk nor sober. Some drink was given to me and to my companions whilst we were knocking down some fences. I don't know who supplied us with the beer.*

MR MIDDLETON: Is it true that you chopped down a tree besides the silver leaved Ivy?

JW: *I chopped down several trees. I did not knock down any iron palings at the gate.*

Mr Shaw objected to this line of examination. The only question before the court was whether Winterburn used the words sworn to by Benson.

MR MIDDLETON to witness: How many people would be employed in the garden pulling down fences and trees?

JW: *About 150.*

MR MIDDLETON: And you say that amongst all these people no violent language was used?

JW: *I heard none.*

Next to take the stand were Joseph Bradley, who worked at the mill with Winterburn, and George Lutey, a mason. Bradley had walked up from the mill to the castle yard with Jack Winterburn around five o'clock. Jack had brought an axe and set about cutting down some of the smaller trees – a young beech tree and a poplar – near the infants' school gates. George Lutey had come up on his own and joined Winterburn at the scene at about twenty past five. When he arrived, Jack was standing by the infants' school doors. The three men went up together to the bower where the ivy was. Joseph Bradley left soon after and went back to work. He'd only been back at work about fifteen minutes when his employer told him to go and fetch Winterburn back too.

He found Jack and George Lutey still where he had left them, near the silver-leaved ivy. A man called Hatley had hold of Jack's arm and was trying to pull him away. Bradley told him "You are to come back to work". After a moment, Jack dropped the axe and said, "I'll come". Hatley let him go.

George Lutey said he'd felt the axe brush against his leg as it fell. He didn't pick it up, although he did stay after Winterburn and Bradley had left. Another witness said they thought they had heard Johnson ask for it and pick it up.

Both Lutey and Bradley categorically denied that Jack Winterburn had said anything like "Stand by or I'll cut thy bloody legs off". They were with him the whole time. If he had said so they would surely have heard him.

One after another, a dozen or more, witnesses came forward all saying the same thing: Winterburn had not touched the ivy; he had never used the words Thomas Benson had claimed; somebody may have said "Chop into it, Jack" but that was not at the ivy, it was when he was chopping down the trees.

John Snowden, Edward Myers and William Haress all gave their statements.

William Burgess, the gardener, summed up by saying "I never heard the words myself used, except by Benson in court."

By the time **stonemason James Flackley** was called to give his evidence it is fair to say he was in a bit of a state. He had dug himself an almighty hole. He wished with all his heart he had not talked to so many people. He wished that he had told everyone the same thing. How was he to keep his story straight now?! He hadn't wanted to come today. He hadn't wanted to give evidence. His mouth was dry. He seemed to have no control over what came out of it. Counsel let him run with it.

It went something like this:

I recall being in Dr Simpson's garden on the afternoon of the riot. I saw Benson and Winterburn there. No, I didn't see anyone do anything to Benson or Burgess. I heard Winterburn say "Stand by or I'll chop your legs off". I'm sure those are the words I heard. I definitely saw Benson there.

He paused for breath.

I know John Kirby junior. I called at John Sweeting's house on the night I got the summons. That's the Green Dragon on Castlegate. I saw John Kirby at Sweeting's before the case was tried at Knaresborough the first time. I haven't seen John Kirby since to speak to. I can't say for sure that I saw Mr Kirby between the first and second examination of the rioters before the magistrates. I may or may not have done so. I didn't tell him that I wished to go as a witness for Winterburn and the other men. I don't remember saying any such thing. My memory is not a long one...

Another pause.

I know a man called Samuel Barrett. We have been very intimate. I remember coming up to Leeds about a fortnight ago. Barrett and I talked about this affair of Benson's. I can't say the day of the month, but it was before I came up to Leeds. We stood talking together for some time in Knaresborough. He asked me if I had heard Jack Winterburn say that he would chop somebody's legs off. I said that I had not. He said, "Well I thought it was a strange thing if you had because during all the time we have been intimate I have never heard you say that you had".

*I don't remember if he asked me if I believed such words had been said by anybody. I didn't say that I believed what Benson had said was all false. Not that I remember anyway. Yes, I was perfectly sober when we had this conversation. I can't swear that I did not say that Benson was speaking falsely. I don't remember saying it. **Benson paid my conduct money for coming here*** *today. When Winterburn said "stand by or I'll chop your legs off", I was close to him. George Lutey was standing next to him and had as good an opportunity of seeing and hearing as I had.*

I told Winterburn himself that I had heard him use these words in Sweeting's taproom a week or two after the riot. I told Sweeting four or five weeks ago.

Re-examined:

I did not want to be a witness here today.

Before the case was first heard by the magistrates, I was examined by Mr Gill. The reason why I said to Barrett I had not heard Winterburn use these words was because I did not want to be called as a witness.

He turned to the courtroom:

When I was first examined by Mr Gill, I did not say that Winterburn had used these words because I did not wish to have anything to do with it.

At this point the magistrates interfered saying that they considered the evidence given for the prosecution insufficient to justify them in sending the defendant for trial upon so serious a charge.

Thomas Benson was discharged.

Dr John Simpson speaks back

To the editor of the Intelligencer

Sir, in your paper of last Saturday you give a very garbled and one sided statement of the case of Thomas Benson of Knaresborough brought up before the Leeds borough magistrates on Tuesday last on an accusation of perjury at the trial at the last Leeds assizes of the men who were convicted of riot and destruction of my property at Knaresborough, and for which the jurors sentenced them, eleven in number, to imprisonment for three months <u>with hard labour</u>.

The case against Benson having failed, the magistrates dismissed it. In your statement, and also in former statements which you have made, not designedly I believe, but because simply you did not know all the facts, you give the public to understand that I have committed some tyrannical and unlawful act, robbing the people of Knaresborough of their rights, and preventing them having access to the banks of the river Nidd and the beautiful scenery in the neighbourhood.

Nothing can be more unfair or untrue. Therefore I think it only just and fair to myself that I should be permitted to make a statement respecting this matter.

The small piece of ground, little more than a rood of land, that I was allowed to enclose from the Crown lands at Knaresborough, adjoined my own property there. It formed a portion of the ground formerly belonging to the Castle but was separated from the Castle yard by the remains of a deep moat. It was filled with rubbish and all kinds of filth and was a disgrace to the town, and most particularly obnoxious to those residing in the neighbourhood. I applied to the owners of the property for release of the same, that I might enclose and beautify it, and do away with such an unseemly nuisance, the property belonging to the Queen as Duchess of Lancaster but being leased to the Duke of Devonshire.

This small piece of ground was leased to me in the year 1855 by the Duke of Devonshire with the licence and consent of the crown at the rent of one pound per annum, when I began to improve it and beautify it, making it a part of my ornamental grounds, and thus spending a considerable sum of money over it. The place was the admiration of all who saw it and added greatly to the beauty of the locality.

The rioters burnt and destroyed a summer house which I had erected, tore down the iron gates and fencing which I had placed, and cut down all the beautiful trees and shrubs which I had planted, which were valued at more than £300, and in fact perfectly destroyed the place; having been actuated to the above outrage by the malevolence and instigation of parties who took good care to remain in the background. The rioters were tried at the last Leeds assizes, found guilty, and *sentenced by Mr Justice Shee to three months imprisonment <u>with hard labour</u>.*

Sir George Grey has since been applied to by some of the friends of the rioters to remit or lessen the sentence, but he has refused to do so, saying that having investigated the case he does not purpose interfering with the sentence passed on the prisoners.

Out of revenge to Thomas Benson for having spoken the truth at Leeds as a witness, his enemies, friends to the rioters, got up a false accusation of perjury against him. The case was heard last Tuesday at Leeds by the magistrates there and was dismissed. Such, Sir, are the leading facts of the case, therefore I hope out of common justice to me you will have the kindness to insert this letter in the next edition of your paper.

I remain yours, &c.,

John Simpson MD, a Magistrate for the West Riding
21 Gloucester Place, Portman Square, London
May 14th, 1866

'The Knaresborough Riot' *Leeds Intelligencer*, 19th May 1866

The tragedies unfold

Meanwhile, back in Wakefield Gaol, the true impact of imprisonment on the Knaresborough Eleven was starting to be felt.

At the time of the trial on the 6th of April 1866, James Fletcher was ill with bronchitis. Conditions in Wakefield Gaol were hardly conducive to an improvement in his health. He deteriorated steadily and was moved into the prison infirmary where, despite several people testifying that he had received good treatment, he died on the 28th of April[15]. He was buried in the church of St John the Baptist in Knaresborough the following day, his grieving widow Jane hardly able to take in the direction events of the last few months had taken.

Just three days later, on the 2nd of May, another heart was broken. William Procter's wife Mary passed away at their cottage down by the Low Bridge. Her death is recorded on the same page of the church register as the burial of James Fletcher.

There was more to come, but that is for later…

---

[15] 'Death of one of the Knaresborough Rioters' *Leeds Intelligencer*, 29 April 1866

Tuesday the 26th of June, 1866...

Freedom for the Knaresborough Eleven - a town in celebration

On Tuesday the 26th of June, the shops in Knaresborough were closed and most of the business of the town suspended. It was a fine sunny day. People were in holiday attire and rushing around making last minute adjustments to their bunting and banners, fixing them in place from window to window across the streets. A platform was erected in the Market Place.

William Mawson, innkeeper at the Black Swan on the High Street and brother of Thomas one of the rioters, and his brother-in-law Edward Myers who ran the Golden Anchor, were amongst several men busy in their kitchens preparing a sumptuous meal from ingredients paid for by the committee.

At mid-morning three brakes[16], drawn by four fine grey horses set off for Harrogate, one carrying the brass band, and another friends and family of the prisoners.

They had learned that the Eleven, or at least nine of them, released that morning, were to be put on a train from Leeds which was due to arrive at Harrogate around noon.

At Harrogate crowds were already gathering around the Station Yard and back into James Street. All along the highway from Harrogate to Knaresborough, people were taking up their places and waiting excitedly.

As the train pulled into Harrogate railway station, the onlookers waved handkerchiefs and cheered loudly. While the men were

---

[16] A brake was a horse-drawn carriage with no sides, just a platform on which men could stand or sit, or goods be transported

taking their seats on one of the brakes, the brass band struck up a tune. Gradually a procession formed: out front several horsemen, then the brake with the brass band, then the carriages with the men and their friends, and a few vehicles carrying friends from Knaresborough taking up the rear. The procession moved off slowly, taking more than an hour to reach Knaresborough, to the sound of enthusiastic cheering all along the way.

On arrival at Knaresborough the throng was so great the procession could barely pass.

> *"The church bells rang a merry peal, handkerchiefs were waved from nearly every window, and flags, banners and streamers bearing mottoes and quotations from scripture were suspended from almost all the available places in the town."*

Two prominent banners in the High Street slung across the full width of the road, said "Welcome to our fellow townsmen" and "Liberty England's Richest Gem". Near the Market Place, there was a piece of calico attached to two poles upon which were written the words "Thou shalt not bear false witness against thy neighbours".

The procession pulled up in the Market Place where Mr Brown took his position on the podium and addressed the returning men.

Valentines Series No. 49042, Knaresborough Market Place c. 1903. Reproduced with permission, from the postcard collection of Isabel Garbutt.

Mr Brown's speech

"Gentlemen – at a meeting of your fellow townsmen and friends, called for the purpose of taking into consideration the best means of giving you a hearty reception, it was unanimously resolved to present you with an address of sympathy on your return home to your families and friends after ending three months unjust imprisonment.

In the first place they wish to express their deep sympathy and condolence with the widow and family of the late James Fletcher, who died during his imprisonment, and that meeting was of opinion that his death was very much accelerated through it. And likewise with William Procter, under the very trying circumstances in which he was placed

37

on the death of his wife, in not having an opportunity of soothing her in her dying moments, and paying the last tribute of affection and respect at her funeral. And to you all they say welcome home and that meeting was unanimous in opinion that you return home not only without a stain on your character, but martyrs in the cause of freedom and liberty; that you were simply defending the rights of the public against the encroachment of Dr Simpson was patent to all the multitude who witnessed the proceedings for which you have so unjustly suffered.

And that meeting wishes to express its dissent to the sentence passed upon you at Leeds, because it was founded alone on the law of riot, without allowing your assertion of the rights of the inhabitants being taken into consideration, which rights were previously given by the judges at York in reference to other proceedings on the same piece of ground.

And that meeting wishes to inform you that you have not been forgotten during your absence, but that your names have been household words among the inhabitants of your town, that they have cared for the wives and families of those who are married; and for you all, in giving you a hearty reception, you will each be presented with a silver cup as a token of esteem, to be handed down by you to future generations, not only to prove that they did not think you guilty of crime, but to testify the abhorrence of the *encroachments of public rights and restraint of public liberty by any person; and that meeting wishes to inform you that your sufferings have not been altogether vain, but have been the means of **forming a society for the opening out of ancient footpaths, and protecting the present from all encroachments,** and one of the rules of that society is that nothing shall be done without legal advice, so as to prevent the malicious propensities of some parties from being gratified by taking criminal proceedings and luxuriating in the idea but they have been the means of depriving some of their fellow townsman of their liberty.*

And that meeting hopes you will live long among us and that your future career will be happy and prosperous."

George Renton's response

George Renton was elected by his fellow rioters to respond to Mr Brown's speech. He did so eloquently and with passion.

"Respectful fellow townspeople it is with much feeling of joy inexpressible that I now have an opportunity of appearing amongst you, freed from the bond of incarceration, or anything that places an obstruction on my liberty. I most particularly wish to impress upon your minds that I consider we are all unblotted by crime or disgrace, as I did before our imprisonment. (cheers)

I beg to thank you most heartily for the most magnificent reception which you have given us on our return to our native town, a reception which is very far beyond the most sanguine expectation of any of us inasmuch as we have done nothing to merit it. All we did was what devolved upon us as true representatives of the free people of this illustrious isle. The only reception we expected was the happy greeting of our dear friends and relations, and your kind verbal sympathy.

It is quite evident from the proceedings of this day that you were desirous of evincing your deep sympathy towards us in a more tangible way, in a manner that would not only leave a lasting impression on our memories and those of our fellow townsmen, but which would also show in every place of this country where newspapers have a circulation your utter abhorrence and entire condemnation of our imprisonment, and your desire to sympathise with us on our return. (cheers)

You most notably contributed to our defence for which I most heartily thank you and I feel proud to say furnished the best counsellors for our defence that we could desire. But from the commencement of the trial, it was evident that nothing short of imprisonment would be our doom.

After our imprisonment you very kindly sent a petition to Sir George Grey desiring him to reduce or commute the sentence, but I never

40

entertained the least idea of its fruitfulness, because the Judge's opinion would be necessary, and it is hardly likely that he would reverse his opinion. But gentlemen your exertions are none the less valued by us because they were unsuccessful. (hear, hear and cheers)

Lastly but not least you most generously subscribed towards providing some weekly allowance for the support of the sorrowing wives and families of the men who had been taken from them. I feel I cannot find words sufficient to express my thanks to you on their behalf, but I am certain that your kindness will never be forgotten by them. (hear, hear)

Whether we were justly or unjustly punished must forever remain an undivulged secret within our breasts. I feel extremely sorry that poor Fletcher and Barker are not with us to participate in this happy meeting, but I hope that Fletcher is now enjoying that everlasting felicity which cannot be equalled by anything on this earth. I trust that your condolences will be the means of soothing the sorrows of his dear relatives. I hope too that ere long Barker will be so far convalescent as to be able to be among us. I feel sure that the deep wound caused in Procter's breast at not being able to be present to witness the last hours of his dear wife will be healed by hearing of your kind sympathy with him.

If those men who so liberally volunteered their assistance for the prosecution perjured themselves for the sake of a conviction and palliated themselves with deceit in this world, at that great day when the secrets of all hearts are made known, when the judge of judges will impartially lay our charges before us, they will then have to answer for that wrong inflicted upon us.

*I freely forgive them, and I **hope that what they would get for their work would supply those wants which I feel sure they are in need of.** (hear, hear)*

Gentleman is not our country looked up to as a pattern nation by all others? Do we not enjoy here privileges which no other country can boast of? Freedom, liberty, and rights are matters indelibly emblazoned on our breasts. Whether a man be rich or poor he will retaliate when he sees his rights usurped and his liberty trampled upon. (cheers)

I feel proud that we have done nothing more than all true Englishmen consider it's their duty to do. (cheers) Although we have been punished for what we did our spirits are not vanquished, we are only more animated with the knowledge of our rights and the desire to enjoy them, and like the true English bulldog though for a time repulsed by punishment for what we have done our spirits can never be subdued. (renewed cheers)

Many nights when I lay sleepless on my comfortless hammock could I rest with far greater content knowing that I had a clear conscience than our convicting friends could at home on their comfortable feather beds with their wives and families. (hear, hear)

*Although **we are not in possession of ill-gotten wealth,** nevertheless our family affections are nonetheless acute, and I feel certain but whatever we may have suffered either mentally or corporately is far preponderated by this enthusiastic reception. (cheers)*

I must not forget to thank the inhabitants and visitors of Harrogate for the hearty welcome they gave us. It was evident that they felt aware of the eye sore and annoyance it would cause them if some selfish individual were to take it into his head to seize a portion of their stray, and be determined by repeated unjust legal proceedings to endeavour to establish some rights to which he could substantiate no really honest or honourable claim. (hear, hear)

***The land which we have fought for belonged to our forefathers, it belongs to us, and I trust now will belong to our posterity for time immemorial.** (loud cheers)*

In conclusion I beg again most humbly to tender our sincere thanks for your many marks of kindness towards us and I hope all who are now present, as well as those who are absent and have our cause at heart, will be blessed with health and longevity, and that you and they will be able to witness the happy school children during their recreation on the ground and to hear the harmonious voices of the juveniles breaking forth in merry shouts and ringing laughter whilst engaged in innocent play to the delight and amusement of themselves and to the entire approval of right minded men. (great cheering)"

The dinner and presentation

The reception party then adjourned to the Town Hall. At two o'clock, William Mawson, Edward Myers and the others who had spent the morning busily preparing a substantial dinner, served the men and around 250 of their guests at their tables.

Everyone's stomachs full, and the tablecloths removed, a small table was brought on to the platform, upon which were set eleven tankards, supplied by TS Gibson, the ironmonger. Mr John White, the Chairman, rose to take the stand. He apologised that the job had fallen to him as a last-minute substitute, the intended incumbent Mr Mountain having been overcome by his feelings and unable to continue. He fervently hoped he could do the occasion justice.

He touched upon the events that had led up to the day's celebrations, and then presented the cups to the men in descending order of age.

Henry Dixon was the first to receive his. He took it in his hands. It was made of silver plate and beautifully embossed with swags. He read the words engraved upon it and was moved more than at any time before in his 62 years. It said,

Presented to Henry Dixon

By his fellow townspeople as a token of their deep sympathy on his having suffered three months imprisonment along with 10 others for alleged rioting in the Castle Yard when

asserting the rights of the public against the
aggression of Dr John Simpson

Knaresborough June 26th 1866

One by one the men were called up to receive their honours. Many of them were lost for words. Thomas Johnson was heard to say that the testimonial was worth SIX months in prison; Thomas Mawson that if anyone else enclosed land belonging to the public and somebody were wanted to pull down the encroachment, they could count on him. The testimony to James Fletcher was accepted by his brother George on behalf of Jane, James's widow.

One man, besides the late James Fletcher, was not present to receive his testimony. 22-year-old Thomas Barker had been taken ill in his prison cell and was not well enough to be released with the others. Everyone wished him a speedy recovery and that he would be able to accept his tankard on his return to Knaresborough.

Renton was again asked to say a few words on behalf of the Eleven. He said he was proud of what he had done, that he prized the tankard more than any present that could have been given him, and that should he live to be married, one of the proudest things he should do would be to pass the tankard down to his children, and request those who came after them do the same, so it would never be forgotten that their sufferings had been unjust.

The presentations over, the proceedings at the Town Hall were closed and the whole company joined in singing the National Anthem.

The Gala

The gala later that evening was a joyous occasion attended by more than 3000 people. The whole event passed without incident. The crowd played games on the liberated land, and a foot race was won by Mr George Gibson who received a cup to the value of three guineas.

Postscript

Twenty-two years later...

On the evening of Monday the 9th of July 1888, the volunteer band under the leadership of Sergeant Instructor Manley gave a musical entertainment in the Castle yard to raise money toward the works then being carried out in connection with the Jubilee scheme for improving the banks. The weather during the evening was very cold and windy and no doubt deterred many from enjoying the music. £1 3s was thrown into the collecting sheet. Promises of contributions from a number of people, together with the nett receipts from the band performance, meant that the work was able to go on a little longer and the committee hoped to complete immediately the riverside portion of the banks. The total amount subscribed for the additional works up to that time was £57 2s[17].

Two of the subscribers that day were Mr Wm Ranson and Mr J Winterburn Mason – Castle Yard rioters.

---

[17] *Knaresborough Post*, 9 July 1888

Part II: The man in the shadows

The law locks up the man or woman
Who steals the goose from off the common,
But leaves the greater villain loose
Who steals the common from off the goose.

The law demands that we atone
When we take things we do not own
But leaves the lords and ladies fine
Who take things that are yours and mine.

The poor and wretched don't escape
If they conspire the law to break;
This must be so but they endure
Those who conspire to make the law.

The law locks up the man or woman
Who steals the goose from off the common
And geese will still a common lack
Till they go and steal it back.

Anonymous, 18th century[18]

William Johnson the Footpath Reformer

There are several references in the newspaper accounts to a man in the background who had something to do with previous incidents at Dr Simpson's grounds. John Simpson himself, in his

---

[18] Boyle, James. "The Second Enclosure Movement and the Construction of the Public Domain." Law and Contemporary Problems, vol. 66, no. 1/2, 2003, pp. 33–74. JSTOR, http://www.jstor.org/stable/20059171 . Accessed 25 Aug. 2022.

letter to the editor of the Leeds Intelligencer, 14th May 1866, mentions *"the malevolence and instigation of parties who took good care to remain in the background"*. So, who was this shadowy character?

At the trial, Superintendent Ormsby reported that he had seen a person named Johnson at the scene. He knew this Johnson had been connected with an earlier disturbance at Castle Yard in 1862. A boy, Benjamin Middleton, identified Ormsby's Johnson as **the brother of Thomas Johnson, the accused**.

On the 26th of June 1866, at the town celebrations, a twelfth tankard was presented, not to one of the rioters but to "William Johnson, **footpath reformer**" for services rendered to the town.

William Johnson, a tailor, had it seems been like a flea biting at the ankles of John Simpson for several years. And not just John Simpson but other landowners as well.

As far back as 1854, the Bradford Observer of May 18th reported that Sir Charles Slingsby had travelled down to London to consult with his lawyer, amongst other things in relation to the actions of "Messrs Johnson and co, **footpath reformers of the Flatt**". The term "flatt" refers to blocks of land with the plough furrows all running in the same direction in the traditional open field system of farming.[19] Johnson alleged that Sir Charles had enclosed the flatt in order to manufacture "faggot votes"[20]. It was clearly a bit of a hot potato - on advice from his lawyers, Sir Charles withdrew all his dozens of writs and paid the defendants' costs.

---

[19] Jennings, B (Ed.). A History of Harrogate and Knaresborough (1970)
[20] According to Wikipedia, in an election where property ownership was a qualification for voting, a faggot voter typically held the title to a subdivision of a larger property with a single beneficial owner. Faggot voting was a common electoral abuse in England until the electoral reforms of the late 19th century.
https://en.wikipedia.org/wiki/Faggot_voter

Clearly recognised as an organised activist, William Johnson was at the leading edge of a movement that still continues today. Mr Brown, chair of the reception committee during Knaresborough's celebrations, told the men that their sufferings had not been altogether in vain but had been the means of **forming a society for the opening out of ancient footpaths and protecting the present from all encroachments**. Formed in response to the 1845 General Enclosure Act in England, local groups campaigning for the rights of "commoners" to continue to use common land and traditional rights of way started forming in the mid-19th century. The Commons Preservation Society was established in 1865, the same year as the Castle Yard riot, merging with the National Footpath Preservation Society in 1899 to form what is now the Open Spaces Society[21]. The National Council of Ramblers' Federations (the forerunner to The Ramblers) arose later from the same political movement in 1931[22].

The Castle Yard footpaths

The concept of a public footpath as a route by which people had a legally protected right to pass and re-pass on foot across otherwise private land had been around for centuries before the Castle Yard affair. Many footpaths in England started out as the traditional routes used by people to reach their church (known as "Mass paths"), to carry coffins to funerals, and to access their places of work. Although technically a footpath was created by the landowner "dedicating" it as a public right of way, in practice the majority had been in place so long the documents recording their dedication no longer existed. Today, in 2022, if a path has been in use by the public unchallenged by the landowner for

---

[21] https://www.oss.org.uk/about-us/our-history/saving-open-spaces-campaigning-for-commons-green-spaces-and-paths/

[22] https://en.wikipedia.org/wiki/The_Ramblers

more than twenty years it is deemed to have been implicitly dedicated as a public right of way, but of course that ruling was not in place in 1865.

Long before Dr Simpson acquired the small strip of land by lease from the Duke of Devonshire in 1855, several such footpaths crossed the Castle Yard, one of which ran from the National School, between Castle Lodge and the Castle ruins, along the line of the moat which Dr Simpson filled in, and down the steep banks to the Waterside below. It is clearly marked on the Ordnance Survey Town Plan, surveyed in 1849 and published in 1851, and in fact is still in use today.

Burgess was not sure where the "natural boundaries" of Dr Simpson's land lay. He knew that the boundaries had been pushed back about 20 yards in 1863 – he himself had helped to do this – and understood that this followed an incident the perpetrators of which had been tried in York, but he knew no details about the trial. The gardener at the time of the previous incident had been John Craggs.

The 'Battle of Knaresborough'

In fact there had been several incidents. On the 12th of October 1859, William Johnson the "footpath reformer" was summoned before the Knaresborough Bench of Magistrates for wilfully breaking the lock of gates attached to a piece of land on the north side of the Castle-yard, enclosed by Dr Simpson, under a lease from the Crown – the same piece of land that was at the heart of the 1865 riot. The Justices convicted and ordered him to pay damages and expenses.

However, Johnson and his colleagues insisted that the traditional right of way over the land during the time it had belonged to the Duchy, overrode the jurisdiction of the magistrates. In January 1860, the case was brought before the Court of Queen's Bench who **overturned the conviction**. Johnson had been served with process but since his case was not brought on for hearing at the next Assizes, he and his assistants broke the lock again on the 19th of July 1860.

This was tried on the 15th of October and was again found in favour of the defendant.

On the 17th of April 1862, Johnson issued a handbill, signed by himself, intimating that he had succeeded in obtaining a final and irrevocable verdict in his favour, and calling upon the inhabitants to celebrate with him by assisting to remove the hated enclosures. This was followed by an anonymous placard, denying that Johnson had obtained a verdict, asserting that Dr Simpson had won the cause, and warning persons against being led into illegal acts. Johnson replied, re-affirming his previous declaration, commenting severely on his anonymous antagonist, and calling upon his fellow townsmen to rally round him on Easter Monday, when he would re-establish the rights of the public.

The Leeds Intelligencer of the 26th of April 1862 took up the story, describing the ensuing action in battle terminology.

"Last Monday morning, therefore, the "eyes of the world" were upon Knaresborough, where every man was expected to do his duty whatever that might be. The town was all excitement from early dawn, and by noon the windows of the courthouse were filled by Justices, and all available policemen were mustered upon the scene of action, so that if necessary, the omnipotence of the law might be vindicated. Along the palisades and gates forming the objectionable boundary fencing were arranged two deep a mass of stalwart fellows, who were to form a guard to protect it from the threat and devastation. In front of them, filling up that part of the Castle-yard,

an immense number of persons had assembled, whose sympathies were evidently with the tailor rather than the doctor.

Johnson marched to the battlefield at one o'clock, with a bodyguard of half a score stout fellows armed with pickaxes. The invaders immediately attacked the iron palisades but were stoutly resisted by the army of occupation.

General Johnson, however, was not baffled. While keeping up a warm skirmish with the defenders of the wall, he took off a detachment, who quietly stole round to the lower part of the wooden fencing, and in a jiffy, yards of it were brought down with a crash. Through this breach the besiegers poured in irresistible numbers, and the work of demolition went rapidly on. Yard by yard the ground was gallantly fought, but the invaders were too numerous to be resisted, and despite the heroism of the garrison, out-work after out-work was carried, and eventually the great gates were won and came down with a crash that made the welkin ring. Cheer upon cheer rose from the dense mass in the Castle-yard in commemoration of the great victory, and the crowd gradually dispersed. The battle of Knaresborough had been won and lost."

Knaresborough Castle c.1906, children playing on the footpath between Castle Lodge and the ruins of the King's Tower. Reproduced with permission, from the postcard collection of Isabel Garbutt.

The disputed land

John Simpson mentions having a house in Knaresborough in his 1825 Journal[23]. He describes showing the wonderful view from his house to a visiting friend. At this stage he is unmarried, living in Bradford as a newly qualified doctor, not yet having acquired his uncle's inheritance which allowed him to live the life of a gentleman.

By the time the land around Knaresborough was being assessed for its tithe apportionment in 1845, Dr Simpson and his family were at Cayton Hall, soon to set up home in London. The tithe map shows him owning around 400 acres at Rillington in Malton, the land that he inherited from his uncle. He was letting the land around his Knaresborough house in separate plots, 10 and 11 to

---

[23] *The Journal of Dr John Simpson of Bradford 1825,* City of Bradford Metropolitan Council Libraries Division, 1981

one John Bake as a garden, and the steep land of plot 9 to three men – William Robinson, Thomas Swalwell and Thomas Whitehead – also for a garden. The land of plots 8, and 14 and 15 towards the waterside, were owned by Sir Charles Slingsby.

The footpath later blocked by Dr Simpson's summer house (described in the court report as being on the Duchy land) is presumably the one shown at the bottom of the map below, which ran from in front of the school playground and behind the castle down to Waterside. The rest of the Castle Yard, was still in the hands of the Duchy of Lancaster (the Crown), leased to the Duke of Devonshire who in turn leased part to John Simpson in 1855.

The silver-leafed ivy, two poplars and a jessamine were on the old bowling green. A mountain ash, rhododendrons, and elms and other trees of 15-20 years growth stood on Sir Charles Slingsby's land.

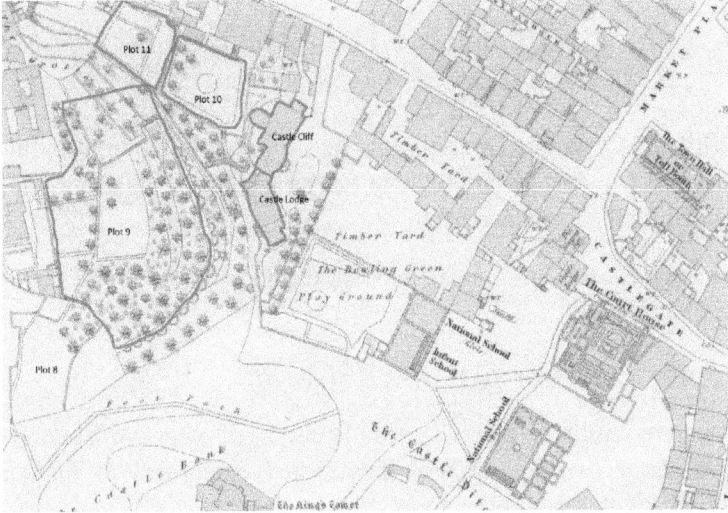

The land belonging to Dr Simpson included Plots, 9, 10 and 11 and the area between Castle Lodge and the infant school playground to just beyond the footpath.

Ordnance Survey Town Plan, Knaresborough Sheet 4. Surveyed 1849; published 1851.
Reproduced and annotated with the permission of the National Library of Scotland.

Part III: The players

Whilst the town celebrations on the 26th of June were a joyful affair, it couldn't be ignored that for three families the event was tinged with sorrow and grief.

These were the families of James Fletcher, Thomas Barker and William Procter.

James Fletcher (1814-1866)

When the riot took place, James Fletcher, a 52-year-old labourer and carter, was living in impoverished conditions in Finkle Street[24] with his wife Jane and their family.

They had been married for nine years but he had lived unmarried with Jane and her children for some years before that, first in Simpson's Yard and then in Screwton's Yard. When they were living there in 1851, Simpson's Yard sounded a sorry place – two of the houses were empty and the other two households occupied by women described as paupers. Jane was the head of the household and James was living with her and the children as a "lodger". The children were at school, Jane was in receipt of poor relief and James brought in a small and unpredictable income as a carter.

Jane's eldest child, William, had been born in 1842. The father's name on his baptism record was given as John Thompson. There is no evidence however that she had ever been married. The year before William was born there were two Jane Thompsons of the right age listed in the Census in Knaresborough – one was a hawker, the other a servant at Conyngham Hall, neither of them married.

---

[24] From his entry in the burials register

56

When her second child Charles was born in 1844, the space for father's name was left empty, as was the case when John was born in 1847. So maybe James had been with Jane since the early 1840s and Charles and John at least were his. Jane and her sister Mary had themselves been illegitimate.

Regardless of the complexities of their legal status, however, they were a family.

Later, after they were married, they lived in Screwton's Yard. The widowed William Screwton, proprietor of land and houses, lived alone in one of the houses. The other two were occupied by James, Jane and their son John, and another married couple. Screwton's Yard isn't explicitly marked on the town plan, but it appears in the Census between Beech Hill and Powell's Yard. James Fletcher's sons Charles and John were much the same age as the rioter Peter Robinson who lived at Powell's Yard so maybe knew him from school.

At the time of the trial on the 6th of April 1866, James was already ill with bronchitis. It was a common problem amongst the poor living in damp conditions. The conditions in Wakefield Gaol were probably not much better. His health rapidly deteriorated and he was moved into the prison infirmary where, in the space of three weeks he lost the battle to live[25].

His body was brought home to Knaresborough the following day and he was buried in the church of St John the Baptist.

There were many expressions of condolence and sympathy at the celebrations in June, James's death having hit the men hard. James had come from a big family with eight brothers and sisters. It was his eldest brother George who received the tankard on behalf of Jane, James's wife.

---

[25] 'Death of one of the Knaresborough rioters' *Leeds Intelligencer,* 28th April 1866

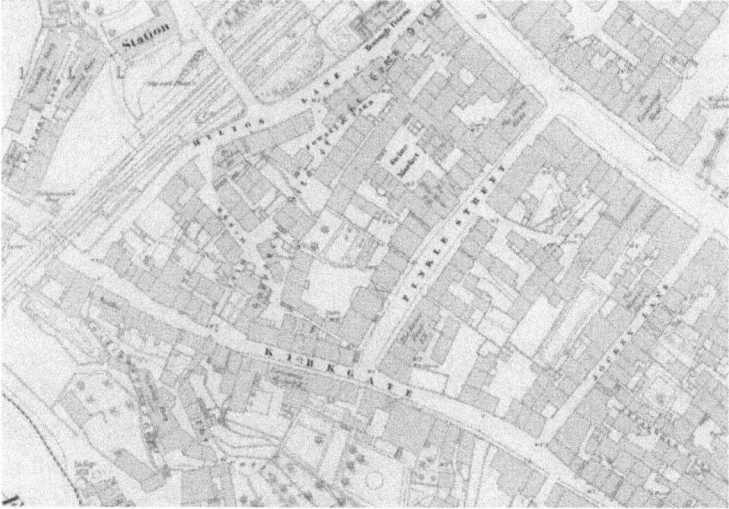

Map showing Finkle Street, where James Fletcher was living at the time of the riot, and Powell's Yard where Peter Robinson lived with his parents and siblings.

Ordnance Survey Town Plan, Knaresborough Sheet 4. Surveyed 1849; published 1851.
Reproduced and annotated with the permission of the National Library of Scotland.

Thomas Barker (1843-1866)

Thomas Barker was the son of cattle farmer Henry Barker and his wife Ann (nee Simpson). He had two little sisters Sarah and Ellen and then a third sister, who died in 1849, almost as soon as she was born, taking his mother with her aged only 28. Mother and baby were buried together on the 3rd of August 1849.

Henry remarried later that year, to Jane Knowles, and went on to have more children, the youngest of whom, George, was only a baby at the time his half-brother was taking part in the riot.

At the age of 7, Thomas, a "farmer's son", was already helping his father in the fields while his sister Sarah, only 4, went to school[26].

By 1861, he was eighteen years old and living-in at the Bay Horse Inn in Goldsborough, working there as a servant. The Yorkshire Gazette in 1865, covering the initial hearing, said Thomas Barker was an ostler looking after the horses of guests staying at the inn. However, in the Schedule of Trials, he is described simply as a labourer, with "imperfect" reading and writing.

After the public meeting on the 3rd of October 1865, which spilled out on to Dr Simpson's grounds, Barker was with Joseph Kearton and Peter Robinson. They were seen setting fire to the summerhouse, with its beech pole supports and ling thatch roof. Some younger children, enjoying the bonfire, dragged branches from some of the trees that had been cut down and stoked the flames further. Sergeant Archy told another of the rioters, Thomas Johnson, he should stop the children from doing this, which he duly did.

When the time came for the men to be released from prison, Thomas Barker was unwell, too ill to leave his cell. Thomas had contracted typhus fever[27]. Sometimes known as "jail fever" because it thrived in overcrowded, unsanitary conditions, typhus was a disease carried by body lice.

He was moved to the Gaol's infirmary, the same infirmary where James Fletcher had died two months earlier. At the celebrations it was expected that he would soon recover and would be able to receive his tankard on his return.

Thomas Barker died aged 22 in Wakefield five days later.

---

[26] 1851 Census – Henry Barker employed one man and one boy, the boy being his seven-year-old son Thomas
[27] Cause of death on his death certificate

It took 11 years for his estate to be wound up, probate eventually being granted to his father and next of kin Henry Barker, Cattle Jobber, on the 4th of August 1877. He left effects valued at less than £200.

William Procter (1809-1887)

William Procter and Mary Fairburn had married in St John's church a few months after James Fletcher and Jane Thompson.

It was the second marriage for both William and Mary. Mary Fairburn already had seven children, and had been pregnant with the youngest – Charles – at the time when her first husband, a poor flax dresser, had died in the summer of 1852. The Fairburns lived on Briggate. Just down the road, also on Briggate, lived the widowed William Procter. His wife of twenty years, Jane (nee Appleton), had been gone for four years. William's children, James and Elizabeth Procter would have gone to school with Mary Fairburn's children.

At the young age of eighteen, William's son James Procter married Mary's daughter Mary Fairburn. Only a few months after their children's wedding, William proposed to Mary and they themselves married on the 2nd of August 1856.

William was a linen bleacher. The family moved up to New York at Summerbridge, just north of Ripley, where there was a flax mill belonging to Francis Thorpe of Knaresborough. They lived in one of the terrace of mill workers' cottages. The mill employed around 150 workers in its heyday. There was work for a linen bleacher, if only on day rates. Mary's teenage daughters also found jobs there. Eventually the family moved back to Knaresborough, into the Union Houses, a row of back-to-back cottages at Calcutt on the far side of the Low Bridge across the river Nidd[28].

Calcutt Houses (previously described as Union Houses or Union Place). Photo reproduced with permission of Tony Newbould.

---

[28] The entry of her burial in the church register gives her place of abode as Union Houses, but the death certificate says she died at an address on Spitalcroft just round the corner.

Mary Procter was only 50 when William, in his prison cell in Wakefield, learned that his wife was sick. She had suffered with heart problems for a year or more, and died four weeks into his sentence. His pain at not being able to sit with her at her sick bed and comfort her, or even to show her the respect of attending her funeral on the 2nd of May, was palpable. Every one of the Knaresborough Eleven felt his suffering along with him.

George Renton in his speech at the town celebrations spoke of the *"deep wound caused in Procter's breast at not being able to be present to witness the last hours of his dear wife"*.

The Chairman of the reception committee also spoke of *"the very trying circumstances in which he [Procter] was placed on the death of his wife in not having the opportunity of soothing her in her dying moments and paying the last tribute of affection and respect at her funeral"*.

Things would never be the same again for the combined family of Procters and Fairburns. Most of the children were old enough to make a new life of their own. The youngest, Charles Fairburn, was 13 when his mother died. He was **taken in by the extended family of John Winterburn**, boarding with linen weaver Samuel Barrick, Winterburn's step-uncle, and working as a linen bleacher like his father.

It's not clear what happened to William himself after the death of Mary and his release from prison. For a while he seems to have disappeared off the face of the earth, no record having been found for him in the 1871 Census. By 1881, at the age of 72, William Procter, former linen bleacher was a pauper inmate at Knaresborough Union Workhouse on Back Lane.

Notice of the death in Knaresborough on the 6th of March of *"William Procter, formerly a linen bleacher"* was printed in the Knaresborough Post on the 12th of March 1887.

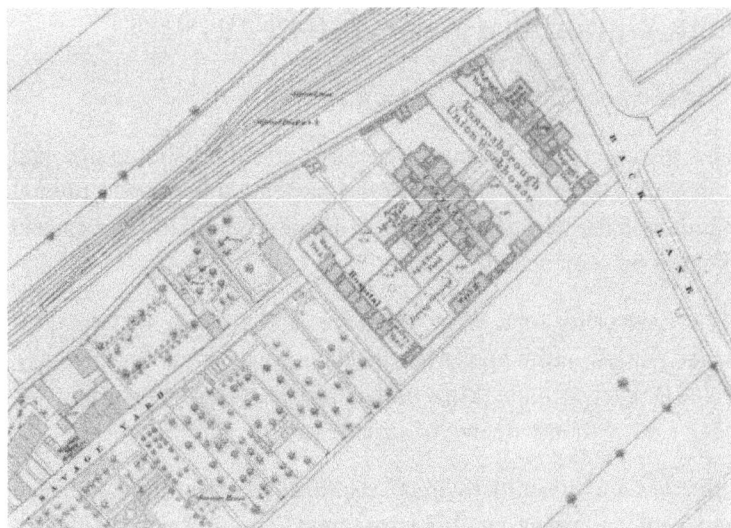

Back Lane workhouse.

Extract from Ordnance Survey Town Plans, Knaresborough - Sheet 3, Surveyed: 1849, Published: 1851. Reproduced with the permission of the National Library of Scotland.

Of the remaining eight men, three – John Winterburn Mason, George Renton and Joseph Harper Kearton – went on to make a significant mark on the newspaper record of the time, each of their lives remarkable in its own way. It is difficult to tell how far this was shaped by their experiences of 1865-6 – their involvement in the Castle Yard riot was never referred to again.

We know less about the others, partly because, with the exception of Peter Robinson, they were older and most of their lives had played out before the riot, and before the establishment of the local newspaper, the Knaresborough Post. Nevertheless, there are things to tell by the more classic family history routes – baptisms, marriages, burials, Census returns, employment records.

Finally, the story would not be complete without touching briefly upon the backgrounds of Dr John Simpson and Mr Justice Shee.

63

John Winterburn Mason (1848-1919)

"Stand off or I'll chop thy bloody legs off!"

The testimony of Thomas Benson that John Winterburn had (allegedly) threatened to cut off the gardener's legs was a pivotal moment in the trial of the Eleven, and the technicality that caused them to be sentenced to prison.

At 17 years old, John Winterburn was still a youth, the youngest of the rioters, and with the hot-headedness of youth he may have made a rash comment. Most of the onlookers thought nothing had been said with any degree of seriousness.

John was a whitesmith by trade, the fine end of working with iron and steel, and other metals such as tin. He used files and lathes to create a polished finish and clean sharp edge, perfect for the mechanisms of machinery. In 1865 at the time of the riot he was employing his skills as a mechanic at one of the linen mills. Throughout his life he spent much time getting to understand the machinery and the workings of the water wheel and how it drove both the linen mill and the pump for the public waterworks.

A family of linen weavers

The linen industry was in his blood.

John Winterburn was the illegitimate son of Mary Winterburn, born in the remote hamlet of West End near Fewston, some three years after the death of her husband George Mason. His birth certificate gives no clue as to his father's name, and he is simply registered as John Winterburn, the Mason part of his surname being added when he was older, maybe when he married.

His mother and her two sisters, Ann and Martha Winterburn, were all power loom weavers. By the time he was 13, his mother and Aunt Martha had moved to Spitalcroft on the far side of the river from the main part of Knaresborough, over the Low Bridge. The women continued to work as weavers and John himself was at school. At the time they lived there, five of the seven households on Spitalcroft were occupied by linen workers.

Spitalcroft was linked by footpaths to a row of back-to-back weavers' cottages on Union Hill. The cottages had cobbled courtyards and communal toilets[29]. One of these cottages was the home of Mary Procter, who died there whilst her husband, the rioter William Procter was serving his sentence.

The year before the Castle Yard affair John's mother Mary married William Barrick. The Barricks lived just over the bridge on Briggate. William's father Joseph was a hand loom weaver, William himself worked on a power loom as did his brother Samuel. Another of their brothers, Thomas had also worked on a power loom before he died some years earlier at the age of 23.

John, having served his sentence and recovered from the excitement of being treated as a hero on his return, settled back into life on Spitalcroft.

In 1869 he married his stepfather's younger sister, Grace Barrick. He and Grace continued to live with Mary and William. Next door was William's brother Samuel with his wife and family. **They had a boarder, Charles Fairburn, a linen bleacher and the youngest son of William and Mary Procter.**

---

[29] https://calcuttvillage.com/about/

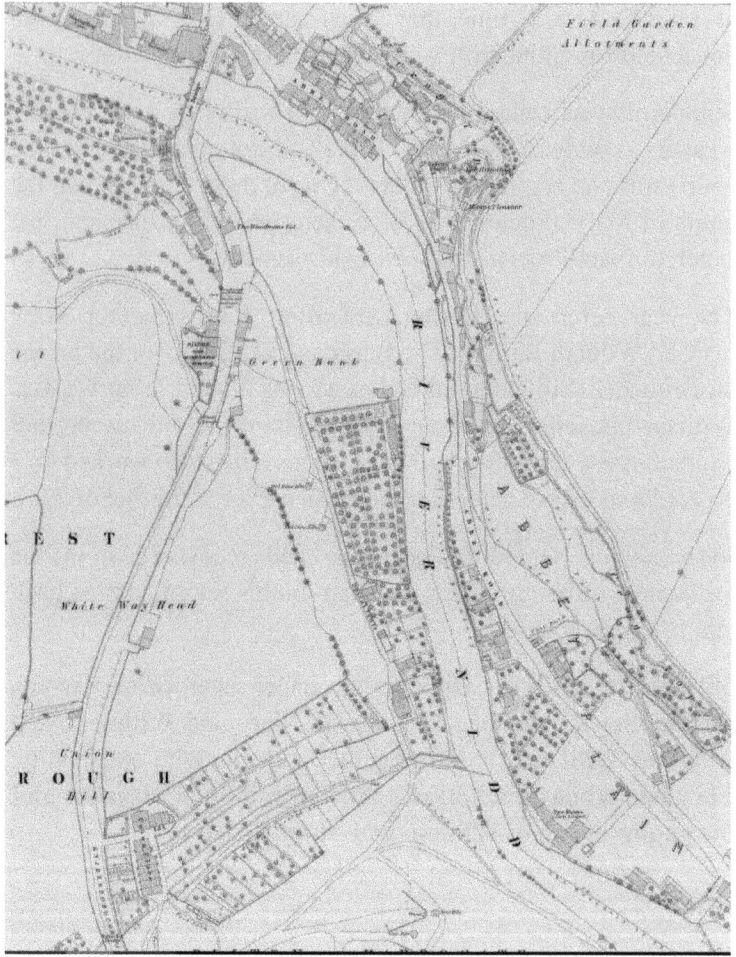

Spitalcroft and the footpaths to the Union Houses in Calcutt

Extract from Ordnance Survey Town Plans, Knaresborough - Sheet 6, Surveyed: 1849, Published: 1849. Reproduced with the permission of the National Library of Scotland.

John Winterburn's marriage to Grace lasted seven years his young wife passing away in the summer of 1876, only in her 30s.

On Christmas Day 1877, he married for a second time. His new wife was Emily Herring, the 18-year-old daughter of James Herring, a power loom weaver, and his wife Rachael. On his marriage certificate he gave his father's name as John Mason, occupation mason. However, this was likely to have been a fabrication for the sake of propriety.

This was to herald a new chapter in his life, one in which he seemed much steadier and more settled.

He moved out from his mother's home in Spitalcroft, and he and Emily rented a 4-roomed cottage of their own at No. 14 Castlegate. John was working as a mechanic on the spring machines at Castle Mill. Their son Harry was born on 11 Mar 1879, followed by another little boy who died as a baby, Mary Alice arrived in 1885 and some while later in 1903 John Winterburn Mason junior was born.

Settled now with a young family, John worked hard, had many of the recreational interests of the working man of the time – fishing, gardening, keeping chickens – and played a full part in community life.

Knaresboro' Star Angling Club

Around the time Harry was born, John Winterburn Mason became involved with the Knaresboro' "Star" Angling Club. Having gone through the Castle Yard affair at such a young age, the notion of standing up for the interests of working men was somewhat ingrained in him. The Star Inn, closed down in 1906 to make way for the entrance to the quarry, was on Abbey Road, on John's way home from work. Its Angling Club set up in 1875 was composed almost entirely of working men, who met together to enjoy an innocent pastime.

"During the existence of the "Star" society as a fishing club the number of members has gradually increased traceable no doubt to the sound basis on which it was established viz. that of fostering a recreation for the working men of Knaresborough irrespective of creed or politics and as such it has prospered."

Knaresborough Post, 9 November 1889, on the occasion of their 15th anniversary supper

Indeed, it is entirely possible that John Winterburn Mason was one of its founding members. The first time the Club is mentioned in the Knaresborough Post is in November 1880 when *Mr Winterburn Mason, "the energetic secretary" read the list of award winners.* John himself came second in the Pike category landing a fish weighing 4lbs 4½ oz.

He was re-elected as secretary for many years, still being reported as such in 1896, and referred to as "our Jack". He was diligent in his role as secretary, often writing letters to the Editor of the Knaresborough Post about issues that were *"prejudicial to the interests of the working men anglers of the town".*

By 1912, in his mid-60s, he was no longer secretary but still won first prize for his Dace.

The Star Inn c. 1903. Reproduced with permission, from the postcard collection of Isabel Garbutt.

The 1882 Fire

In June 1882, a massive fire broke out at the premises of Mr Henry Stockdale, spirit merchant, leather cutter, and dealer in all kinds of saddlery, harnesses etc.

> *"Although it is rather invidious to mention in words of praise one man above another in cases of this kind, yet we cannot overlook the valuable assistance rendered by Mr JW Mason of Castlegate and Mr Abel Mason of Bond Street, in the skillful and judicious direction of the hose."*

Knaresborough Post, 24 June 1882

Knaresborough Floral and Horticultural Show

On Thursday the 30th of August 1888 the Knaresborough Floral and Horticultural Show was held, in the grounds of Conyngham Hall, for the first time in ten years. People came from many miles around by train and bus, both to exhibit and to visit.

John and Emily's little garden on Castlegate must have been a picture. They entered exhibits in both the Amateur and Cottager/Artisan classes. Jno. Wint. Mason won prizes for cut flowers in a bouquet for the hand, 2nd place for gooseberries, 2nd place for spring onions, competing against exhibitors from Poppleton, Wetherby and Spofforth[30]. And over the following two or three years saw success with dahlias, asters, and stocks, and for kidney potatoes, cabbages, red celery and onions.

Bolstered by his success with the flowers and vegetables, in Nov 1904, John entered some of his chickens into the Knaresborough Fanciers' Show. The following year his leghorn hen won 2nd prize.

NER Ambulance Class

On the 12th of December 1897 the North Eastern Railway held an ambulance class in the large waiting room of Knaresborough station. John Winterburn Mason, attending the class, proposed a resolution that the class should be opened out to any of Knaresborough's young men who would like to learn how to apply first aid to the injured. The proposal was then extended to invite members of the police force to join the class.[31]

Councillor John Winterburn Mason

Walton's linen works at Castle Mill shared some of its facilities with the Urban District Council's waterworks, including the all-important water wheel, which drove both the mill machinery and the pumps for the town's water supply. At a council meeting in 1895, it was reported in the Knaresborough Post that Walton's linen mill paid a rent of £120 for Castle Mill and that the Council gave them around £125 to rent the place and keep it repaired.

---

[30] 'Knaresborough Floral Horticultural and Fanciers Show' *Knaresborough Post*, 1 September 1888

[31] 'NER Ambulance Class' *Knaresborough Post*, 18 December 1897

The water wheel had broken down back in January and had now collapsed again on Easter Sunday.

On the 27th of April, John Winterburn Mason, who had spent many months over the years working on the machinery at Castle Mills, saw fit to write a letter to the editor of the Knaresborough Post, explaining what he saw as the root cause of the problem.

"Sir - "just another breakdown" (so says The Native in last week's Post). Such reports, without giving the cause are very misleading to your readers, as it was not the bad state of the machinery, or repairing the old with new, that caused the breakdown on Easter Sunday, but the extra weight put on the pumps by speeding them and putting a 12-inch bolt on to a 10-inch pulley, which made it collapse. It was known to be too light, and a new one had been in the yard three weeks ready to put on, but it would not fix itself.

It is a wonder the water wheel had not collapsed before now through neglect in not looking after it, as it has not been thoroughly examined this year, where formerly it was done once a month. The bad condition of the wheel, and extra power taken by speeding the pumps, causes the clows to open 18¾ inches instead of 11 inches to get the same speed.

The water wheel has not lost a tooth, but the next segment to the one that came off in January has, through not having the new one put on. Now, Sir, if the broken wheel and segment had been replaced in January at a cost of about £14 it would have saved the town £40 or £50, besides putting the new shaft to work the pumps in case of breakdowns; and the wheel and two segments now will have to be put on still, or the town will be without water half the summer if it is a dry one, as the pumps cannot work now without running Messrs Walton and Co's machinery.

Just a word or two about the turbine and new cistern. If the council had adopted the scheme that was before them a few years ago, they would have had two strings to their bow instead of one in case of breakdown, and would have been able to keep the present cisterns full of water night and day, without having to get a new one that will only give the extra pressure for one day's supply; and two turbines will give less trouble and better results than one.

Thanking you in anticipation.

I remain, yours respectfully
JW Mason, Castlegate, Knaresborough"

Knaresborough Post, 27 April 1895

The immediate upshot of this seems to have been the election of the said Mr JW Mason of Castlegate to the Knaresborough Urban District Council.

He was assigned to the Finance Committee and the Gas and Water Committee where it was immediately evident that his inside knowledge of the mill and waterworks machinery was indispensable. He quickly became Chairman of the Gas and Water Committee. Where some of his Council colleagues wanted to disentangle the Council's interests from those of Messrs

Walton, John repeatedly argued the symbiotic nature of the relationship.

> *"MR MASON: You are connected with Waltons' mill. If they think proper, they can disconnect you and the town will be without water.*   *[...]*
> *MR NEEDHAM: Mr Mason knows more about the thing than all of us put together"[32]*

At the meeting on the 27th of April 1897, John Winterburn Mason was re-elected as chair of the Gas and Water Committee, narrowly beating Councillor Bramall (3:2 votes).

Whilst his extensive knowledge of the waterworks machinery was acknowledged (although not always liked) by all, in other issues he fared less well. In March 1900, he strongly opposed the opening of the Castle to visitors on Sundays, as a man should not be expected to work 7 days a week. This was hotly debated.

He remained a Councillor until at least 1901.

He nevertheless retained an interest in the Council's business and in July 1902 wrote another letter to the editor of the Knaresborough Post, this time concerning the gas works, signed as JW Mason of Mill House.

Mill House, Waterside

John, Emily and Harry and Mary Alice had moved into the Mill House on Waterside (described in the electoral register as "near Castle Mill from Castlegate") around 1897. Harry inherited his father's love of mill machinery and was working as a millwright.

Joseph, the youngest of the Barrick boys, and brother to John's first wife Grace and his step-father William Barrick, also lived on Waterside and was foreman of the Gas Works.

---

[32] 'Gas and Water Committee' *Knaresborough Post,* 13 June 1896

John Winterburn Mason died in the spring of 1919 at the age of 71.

Walton's Linen Mill and Marigold House Boat c.1912. Reproduced with permission, from the postcard collection of Isabel Garbutt.

Employees of the Gas Works, pre-1914. Reproduced with permission, from the postcard collection of Isabel Garbutt.

George Renton (1845-1923)

George Renton, the young man who, it seems, led the action in Dr Simpson's grounds, was the son of William Jeffrey Renton, a master tailor and draper on the High Street, and Ann Mainman, daughter of a linen manufacturer.

As small children, he and his sister and brothers must have often played on the open grounds around Castle Yard near their grandfather George Renton senior's home at the Sheriff's office.

George's maiden Aunt Elizabeth, a school mistress, appears to have always lived with them and shared the running of the house[33]. In 1859 when he was 14, his mother, herself still in her 30s, died. Elizabeth Mainman stepped up as housekeeper and kept the family together.

The children were encouraged in their studies and in 1865 George's brother William headed off to University in Durham. He returned a few years later a licentiate of the London Society of Apothecaries.

While his sister and brothers remained at home with his aunt and father, (Richard and Thomas eventually continuing the family business after their father's death), young George went to live with his grandparents.

---

[33] Elizabeth Mainman remained unmarried and was recorded as being a schoolmistress in the Censuses of 1851, 1871, 1881 and 1891 (by which time she was 75 years old). In the 1861 Census she was recorded as housekeeper. Her sister had not long since died and she was caring for the family, with the exception of George who had moved in with his grandparents. White's Directory, published in 1866 lists the Grammar School, the National School, the Charity School, the Roman Catholic school and a number of individuals. Elizabeth Mainman is not among them, so we don't know where she taught. If it were at the infants' school in Castle Yard, that would have been an additional motivation for George Renton's involvement in the Castle Yard affair.

George Renton senior was a man well-respected in the community and known by all. Born in 1797, he had been an auctioneer and valuer from a young man and knew everything there was to know about the land and estate around Knaresborough. Advertisements from the 1860s describe Renton and Renton as being the oldest-established and most experienced auctioneers in the district, in operation for nearly 40 years.

What seems to have driven him, though, was a desire to serve his community. By at least 1829, he and his wife Jane were living at the Sheriff's Office in Castle Yard, and alongside his business as an auctioneer, George Renton Snr. was keeper of the Forest of Knaresborough Debtors' prison. In 1841 he took over the role of Sheriff's Officer following the death of Richard Simpson (no relation to Dr Simpson) and was still carrying out this role as an elderly man of 87!

In the 1830s, George Renton Snr. was also appointed by the Improvement Commissioners as collector of rates. He continued to do this for some 30 years, during which time local government underwent considerable change, as a result amongst other things of the Public Health Act of 1848 and the Local Government Act of 1858. The outcome was an amalgamation of the roles of the Local Health Board and the Improvement Commissioners. This increase in responsibility was discussed at length at the Board meeting on the 1st of May 1876.

> *"Mr. Smith said he had been clerk to the Board for some 35 or 36 years. In the first instance they had simply an Improvement rate. Six or seven years ago, when the Local Government Act was adopted, the repair of the roads within the district fell upon the Board. The duties of the officers and the business of the Board then became in a very different position. Previously he had had a salary as clerk of £30 a year, and the*

collector £15. Mr Renton was collector somewhat over 30 years when he felt the duties were insufficiently remunerated, and gave them up, after the adoption of the Local Government Act. The question of salaries came before the Board, and Mr G. Renton, Jun., came on behalf of his grandfather to ask for an increase of salary as collector. His (Mr Smith's) salary as clerk was advanced from £30 to £60 a year and Mr Renton, as collector, from £15 to £30.

After the adoption of the Local Government Board, they became possessed of the waterworks, and there was additional work in connection with that; and he (Mr. Smith) asked for an increase in salary. He had no doubt the question of salaries was thoroughly sifted then, and he was given an advance of over £30 on account of the waterworks, of which property he had the care and superintendence. An additional sum of £25 was given to the collector, making his salary £55 pounds and his (Mr Smith's) £90. The surveyor received 30s a week, and the same committee that gave him (Mr. Smith) £30 for the waterworks, said he (the surveyor) should have £5 for general superintendence of the waterworks, and his house rent free. The medical officer and sanitary inspector then came into office, the medical officer with a salary of £60 a year and the sanitary inspector £30; half of which they got back from the government."

The Knaresborough Post, 6 May 1876

The Medical Officer of Health at that time (May 1876) was Dr William Renton, George junior's brother. Edwin Smith, clerk to the Improvement Commissioners and clerk to the Board of Guardians for 40 or more years, was Dr Simpson's neighbour living next door at Castle Cliff.

Returning to the story, George Renton senior was particularly fond of his grandson George and clearly fostered in him a passion for auctioneering, an understanding of the laws surrounding the land, and a set of values which included standing up for what you believed to be right. George finished his schooling and was taken on as a surveyor's assistant.

In 1865, the year of the riot, he reached the age of 20. It was a year when his upbringing and the influence of his grandfather would carry him through the most challenging of times. In the January his father William Jeffrey Renton died; his brother William was away at university and his other brothers were finding their feet running the family drapery business.

Living as he did in the Castle Yard, he must have been very aware of the growing discontent in the town at the encroachments of magistrate Dr John Simpson from London. He would have seen first-hand the incident a few years previously when four men had been indicted for riot whilst trying to take down the said John Simpson's fences.

On the 3rd of October 1865 he and his grandfather were present at the public meeting to discuss Dr Simpson's complaints about the noise from the Infants School. As the meeting finished and people spilled out into the Yard young George Renton put it to the crowd that since the land had belonged to the people of Knaresborough, they should maybe consider taking it back. He led and others followed, he tried the gates, and Burgess the gardener who had seen them approaching told him that they were unfastened.

Renton said that although he did not himself cause any damage, he was proud of his part in the action. Several police witnesses saw him bring a pitcher of beer down to the men and offer continued encouragement.

Later, when he and the other men were incarcerated in Wakefield Gaol, he received a visit from his grandfather, telling him of the petition the Town's elders had sent to Sir George Grey, signed by more than a thousand people, and reassuring him that on their release they would be treated as heroes. It was not normal practice to receive visits. George Renton senior's, position as Sheriff's Officer undoubtedly lent weight to his request.

The young George Renton was well-educated (on the Schedule of Trials only he and Joseph Kearton were recorded as being able to read and write "well", the others all "imperfectly") and the men elected Renton to speak on their behalf at the welcome home ceremony. He spoke with eloquence.

Afterwards

By the time of their return, Dr Simpson had put his boundaries back where they should be, and life apparently continued as it had before.

In 1868, the first references to "Renton and Renton" auctioneers, surveyors and valuers – a joint business between George senior and George junior – start to appear in the local newspapers. George Renton senior had been in business, operating from the Castle Yard, since the 1820s.

Grandfather and grandson were undoubtedly a formidable pair. The loss of Jane Renton, George junior's grandmother, in 1869 can only have brought the two men closer together. In 1874, they were elected together to the Board of Commissioners.

On the 28th of November 1878, George married Rose Bertha Shutt, the daughter of Isaac Thomas Shutt, architect, auctioneer, farmer and sometime owner of the Old Swan in Harrogate. The couple married by licence at St Peter's Church. George and his young wife moved to Harrogate and set up home at No. 2, Grove Villas, Queen Parade.

For George senior, now an old man, this must have left a big hole in his life. However, in the 1881 Census he had **living with him, employed as his servant, Hannah Johnson the daughter of Thomas Johnson who had been a baby at the time of the riot**. He died in 1885, leaving £1996 11s (worth about £273,287 in 2022) to his grandson.

Rose's father died just a few months after they married.

They had five sons and one daughter. The middle son, Theodore Rolande Victor Renton worked for his father and carried on the land agent business. Claude Lucien William Renton and Elwyn George Renton both died in WWI. Elwyn George died at Lahore, Punjab, India on 29 May 1918 and is buried at Karachi, Pakistan. Marie Blanche Renton also died during the War.

George Renton, Castle Yard rioter, himself, died on 23 November 1923 and is buried at Harlow Hill cemetery.

Joseph Harper Kearton (1848-1914)

Of all the Knaresborough Eleven, it was Joseph Kearton whose achievements went on to receive the greatest acclaim. Whilst Jack Winterburn Mason and George Renton undoubtedly made significant contributions in their home town, the name Joseph Harper Kearton became recognised throughout the length and breadth of England.

Joseph was born on the 25th of October 1848, the third of George and Ann Kearton's four children and their only son. His parents met whilst in service for the Rev. Thomas Collins, curate of Farnham, at what is now known as Knaresborough House[34]. George Kearton was the footman and Ann Harper a housemaid. They married in 1843 when Joseph's mother was 22 years old and moved into a home of their own on Bond End.

It was clear from an early age that Joseph was a very bright child and had an unstoppable passion for music. Maybe encouraged by the Rev. Collins, he was already singing as a little boy when the new Holy Trinity church was being constructed. Built on land provided by the Slingsby family, the new church provided an extra 612 free seats to accommodate the town's growing population of linen workers. When it opened its doors for the first time in 1856, seven-year-old Joseph Kearton was part of its very first choir.

His father does not seem to have been a strong presence in the little boy's life. In 1854 George Kearton was no longer working as a footman, and is listed in the 1854 Directory of Leeds as running a beerhouse on Knaresborough High Street.

---

[34] The Knaresborough Town Council offices. The house had been built around 1768 for an earlier Rev.Thomas Collins, vicar of Knaresborough, and remained the home of the Collins family until bought by Knaresborough Urban District Council in 1951.

By the time of the 1861 Census, George had moved out of the family home and returned to his home village of Kirkby Malzeard, he and his brother Richard working as labourers for their cousin Sarah, who is described in the census as a landed proprietor.

Meanwhile Ann is recorded as head of the household and was living in Jockey Lane with the children. Periodically Ann Kearton received Poor Relief of 2/6d for her children. She worked as a dressmaker and milliner, helped by Joseph's eldest sister Alice. The two younger girls were still at school. Joseph, only 12 years old had a job himself, as a clerk.

It was probably around this time that his mother made the decision to put her marriage behind her and she started a new life with one Thomas Corker, a master tailor ten years younger than herself. In White's Directory of 1866, Thomas Corker is listed as a tailor on the High Street, and Ann Corker had her own millinery business in the Market Place. There is no evidence that she and Thomas ever married – after all her husband George Kearton was still alive, if absent. But she and her youngest daughter Elizabeth moved in with Thomas, she called herself Mrs Corker and was still using that name until she herself died more than 20 years later. In the 1891 Census, Elizabeth Kearton, still a spinster, is recorded as the adopted daughter of Thomas Corker the tailor. After the death of Thomas Corker in the 1890s, Elizabeth Kearton ran the tobacconist's on the High Street, shown in the photograph below.

Knaresborough High Street c.1902. Reproduced with permission, from the postcard collection of Isabel Garbutt

The Castle Yard affair

Around the time of the Castle Yard affair, Joseph Kearton had been appointed as organist at the Congregational Church and was taking on music pupils. He was still only 17 years old, although the Calendar of Trials has him as eighteen.

His involvement in the dismantling of Dr Simpson's encroachments was probably opportunistic. Thankfully, his conviction for this did not however seem to impact much on his budding musical career. He soon became a tenor singer at York Minster under the tutelage of Mr Howard Herring, the organist at St Helen's, York, with additional help from Dr EG Monk who was keen to see Joseph do well.

Wells Cathedral

Kearton's time at York was fairly short lived. Offered a vicar-choralship at Wells Cathedral, in 1868 he left his native Yorkshire for Somerset. There he met Caroline Coles, daughter of yeoman farmer John Coles. He and Caroline married at St

Cuthbert's in Wells on the 10th of January 1870. They set up home at 9 Vicars Close, where they employed a 14-year-old servant called Eliza Williams.

Alongside his commitments at the cathedral, Joseph was intent on developing his musical career. His potential was clear for all to see. Using the professional name of J Harper Kearton, he was appointed music member at Wells grammar school and at St Anne's school Haltonborough, professor of singing at Downsdale college near Bath, and organist at Crescombe. In between engagements he set aside time to continue his music studies under Mr Edward Herbert, at that time organist at Sherbourne Abbey.

He took his studies seriously and kept his eyes on the goal of a career as an organist, composer and teacher. In 1871 he passed his first exam towards the degree of Mus. Bac. Oxon. It was his singing however that started to draw attention. Alfred Stone, editor of *The Bristol Tune Book*, advised him to enrol at the Royal Academy of Music, London, as a vocal student, where one of his tutors was Sir Arthur Sullivan of Gilbert and Sullivan fame. He grasped every opportunity he could to further his knowledge and improve his skills, funding his short time there through numerous concert and singing engagements.

Westminster Abbey

The hard work paid off and in 1877, Joseph Harper Kearton won the prestigious position as one of twelve vicars choral at Westminster Abbey under the direction of Westminster Abbey organist and Master of Choristers Sir John Frederick Bridge.

Caroline and Joseph had their first four children whilst they were living at Wells. The family now packed up their home and moved to 2 Cleveland Villas, Northcote Road, Battersea.

Kearton was amongst the choristers singing at all the major services around the turn of the century including Queen

Victoria's Golden Jubilee, and the coronation of King Edward VII. The pinnacle of his Westminster Abbey career however must surely have been the great honour of being chosen to sing the tenor solo in the Prince Consort's *Te Deum Laudamus* in front of Her Majesty at her Golden Jubilee thanksgiving on the 21st of June 1887.

> *God save the Queen was played & then changed to Handel's Occasional Overture, as I was led slowly up the Nave & Choir, which looked beautiful all filled with people. I sat alone oh! without my beloved Husband (for whom this would have been such a proud day!). The service was very well done & arranged. The 'Te Deum' by my darling Albert sounded beautiful*[35]

The Te Deum Laudamus by Prince Albert of Saxe-Coburg and Gotha (1819-1861) was composed for performance in Westminster Abbey in 1845 and recorded for the first time by the singers of Holy Trinity, Brussels, in 2021.

https://www.youtube.com/watch?v=t116hn6t0fM

The tenor part as would have been sung by Joseph Harper Kearton
https://www.youtube.com/watch?v=piHZsg2USxM

The manuscript is held at the British Library and can be viewed online   at
https://www.bl.uk/manuscripts/Viewer.aspx?ref=r.m.21.e.24_fs 001r

---

[35] Her Majesty Queen Victoria in her diary account of the day of her Golden Jubilee
https://en.wikipedia.org/wiki/Golden_Jubilee_of_Queen_Victoria

J Harper Kearton, the celebrated tenor

Not long after his appointment at Westminster Abbey, Kearton secured an audience with Ebenezer Prout who set him off on a highly successful career as a concert vocalist. Prout engaged him for his high-class concerts at the Borough of Hackney Choral Association. From there he went from strength to strength, appearing season after season at Mr Mann's famous Monday and Saturday popular concerts at the Crystal Palace, the Covent Garden promenade concerts, the Bristol, Chester and Hereford festivals, and many others.

At the beginning of his success, in December 1877, Mr J Harper Kearton returned as a guest vocalist to his home town of Knaresborough where his friends and former colleagues of the choir at Holy Trinity church were singing Handel's Messiah at the Town Hall[36].

As his reputation spread, the newspapers were full of praise.

> *The third of the series of popular concerts took place at the Park Hall [Cardiff] on Saturday evening [...] Interest centred chiefly in Mr Harper Kearton, solo tenor of Westminster Abbey, a singer whose unquestionable powers both voice and expression it would have been quite impossible for the coldest audience not to recognise and appreciate. Each and all of his songs were admirably given and it is therefore all the more to be regretted that so large a number of the patrons of music in Cardiff missed [due to the inclement weather] the pleasure of hearing one of the*

---

[36] 'The "Messiah" at Knaresbro' *Knaresborough Post* 22 December 1877

purest and sweetest tenors in the English platform[37]

One has to search quite hard to find a negative review. Of course, everyone has the occasional off day! In November 1886 his performance of Dvorjak's *The Spectre's Bride,* a notoriously tricky work, had failed to impress the writer of a review in *The Lute* who felt *"Mr Harper Kearton sadly lacked warmth and dramatic fire"* [38].

Kearton was not going to let that happen twice, and in the following May, *The Musical World* said of a different performance of the same work *"Mr Harper Kearton possesses a genuine and sympathetic tenor voice, excellent method, artistic delivery, and indeed deserves the warmest recognition"*[39].

The Westminster Glee Singers

From the early 1890s, when it has to be remembered he was still only in his 40s, Joseph was often to be found singing with a quartet, a style which clearly suited him. The first few performances were made up of different combinations of vocalists, but eventually the Westminster Glee Singers was born. Comprising Joseph Harper Kearton and another lay vicar from the Abbey, Charles Ackerman, together with two vocalists from the Chapel Royal, Walter Coward and William H Brereton, the group's entertaining and often humorous offering was highly sought after. A quick search of the British Newspaper Archive using the terms "Kearton" and "westminster singers" yields nearly 450 results!

---

[37] The Cardiff popular concerts, *South Wales Daily News* 28 November 1892

[38]'From the provinces – Bristol' *The Lute*, 1 Jun 1886

[39] Quoted in the *Knaresborough Post's* biography of him on 10 Nov 1888

The Westminster Glee Singers were universally well-received, as this review of an August Bank Holiday concert in Dover shows.

> *The showery weather on Monday made outdoor entertainments impossible, and the promenade concert with which the week's entertainments opened was held in the Town Hall instead of the Dover College grounds. The attendance was small, the body of the hall being almost empty. But although the audience was very small it was enthusiastic, the programme being an excellent one. It was shared by the Royal Artillery band and the Westminster Glee Singers a male quartette who have musical talent and entertaining charm. It was their first appearance in Dover and they scored an instant success. Their repertoire was very varied, included in it being several humorous numbers, which were sung in a manner which won them unanimous encores. The march "The Mulligan Musketeers" was particularly well sung, and another pleasing number was the negro melody "Old Joe". Several dainty song dances were also given with effect[40].*

On Thursday the 13th of October 1898, the Westminster Glee Singers sang Kearton's own arrangement of *Drink to Me Only with Thine Eyes* at the World's Greatest Classical Music Festival – the Proms at the Royal Albert Hall[41]

---

[40] 'Westminster Glee Singers and Royal Artillery Band concert' *Dover Express,* 29 August 1909

[41] The Proms, https://www.bbc.co.uk/events/ec2p5v

Musical works

Less well-known was the fact that Joseph Harper Kearton was himself an accomplished composer of vocal and instrumental pieces, as his biography in the Knaresborough Post in 1888 shows[42].

Weekes & Co. published six Organ Voluntaries of his; Marshall & Co. published *"The Children's Harvest Song"*; a duet, *"Stars of the Summer Night"* set to the lyrics of Henry Wadsworth Longfellow's poem of the same name, was published by Evans & Co. His anthem *"Blessed Are the Merciful"*, published by Pitman, was frequently sung at Westminster Abbey, St George's Chapel Royal at Windsor and Wells Cathedral, as was *"An Evening Service in G"*.

One of his works may be familiar today to viewers of the BBC production of *Jane Eyre (2011)*. Included in the soundtrack is a piece called *Farewell* written in 1874, words by Lord Byron, music by Joseph Harper Kearton, arranged by Andrew McKenna and performed by Imogen Poots[43]

Retirement

Eventually it seems that the emotional rollercoasters of Joseph Harper Kearton's life and the intense pursuit of his musical career started to take their toll. Somewhen around 1906 he developed a throat infection which progressed into a severe attack of rheumatic fever[44]. The long-term effects of this were devastating

---

[42] 'Yorkshire musicians – Kearton' *Knaresborough Post*, 10 November 1888

[43] https://www.imdb.com/title/tt1229822/soundtrack

[44] The notices of his death in 1914 in many of England's newspapers around England say he had been an invalid for nearly eight years

to his singing career and he cut back his commitments, focussing mainly on his engagements with the Westminster Glee Singers.

At the time of the 1911 Census, Caroline Kearton, now aged 63, and two of her six surviving children, now grown up, were living in Braywood Avenue, Egham. Joseph was not with them. Identifiable only by his initials, age, place of birth and occupation – retired vocalist – he can be found in the Census as in inmate at Holloway Sanatorium 3 miles away in Virginia Water, an institution for patients suffering from temporary episodes of mental illness[45].

One of the side effects of rheumatic fever, although mainly affecting children, is a condition called Sydenham chorea. This manifests itself in twitches and tics, obsessive-compulsive disorder, and a tendency to cry a lot or laugh inappropriately. Maybe Joseph Harper Kearton was afflicted with this. Or maybe he was just burnt out.

Holloway Sanatorium was a new concept, neither a pauper asylum nor a private care establishment for the rich, it was a facility for the middle classes who were temporarily deranged, its aim to help "the professional breadwinner whose income ceases when he is unable to work". It was known for its innovative approaches such as massage and exercise therapies. By the time Joseph Harper Kearton was resident there, the sanatorium had 368 inmates and 227 resident staff.

The cost of staying at Holloway may have been a bit much. On the 13th of March 1912 Joseph Harper Kearton was admitted to Graylingwell Hospital, the West Sussex County Asylum, where he remained until on the 28th of February the following year he was discharged, apparently recovered.

---

[45] https://en.wikipedia.org/wiki/Holloway_Sanatorium

He was in no way abandoned by his family during this period. For both his stay at Holloway and his time at Graylingwell, Caroline and the children were living nearby.

He came home to their house at Southwick near Brighton but died there less than a year later and was buried in Southwick on 10 February 1914. Newspapers all over the country carried notices of his death and recalled with fondness times when the celebrated tenor had performed for them.

The musical Kearton family

It would be interesting to know if Joseph's not inconsiderable talents were present in George Kearton, Ann Harper or any of their ancestors.

Certainly, every one of Caroline and Joseph's six surviving children possessed the gift to a greater or lesser degree. Little Frederick Powell Kearton didn't live to develop his. Born a few months after the family's move to London, he passed away aged 2½. Cecil was not a performer, but he did have a musical ear and perfect pitch, and became a tuner of musical instruments, living for much of his life with his sister Edith. Although Arthur did not make a career from music – he was clerk to a Church Society and then trained in his 30s to be a solicitor – he did have a fine voice.

On Thursday the 3rd of November 1893, Joseph's son Arthur and daughter Annie sang with him at a Grand Concert in the Castle Assembly Rooms in Brentford. Arthur Kearton was in excellent voice and *"pleased so greatly that an encore was demanded and acknowledged"* [46]. It was Annie's debut as a soprano vocalist (mentioned in the British Musical Biography) and she was

---

[46] 'Mr GM Fermor's Concert' *Middlesex Independent*, 18 November 1893

reported as being a little nervous, but nonetheless gained liberal applause.

At their next engagement together – the annual Choral Union concert held at the Clarendon Hall in Watford on the 4th of December, Annie had gained confidence, singing several items on the programme[47]. *"To Miss Annie Kearton were entrusted the soprano soli, and that lady was loudly applauded for all her performances. Her voice is singularly rich and clear and possesses a fineness which cannot fail to carry an audience with it"*. Her sister Edith was a last-minute substitute for one solo which *"was sufficient to show that she also possessed a splendid voice"*.

Two months later, Annie (soprano), Edith (contralto) and Harper (tenor) sang at Andover Town Hall, accompanied by the girls' youngest sister, Helen Kearton aged 10½, on the violin.

> *The head of this family, Mr. Harper Kearton, (principal tenor, Westminster Abbey) had already made his bow to an Andover audience, but on this occasion, he introduced his three daughters Miss Annie Kearton (soprano), Miss Edith Kearton (contralto), and Miss Helen Kearton (violin). According to their capacities, each of these performers succeeded in securing the appreciation of the company. A welcome as between old friends was accorded Mr Kearton whose pure liquid voice was in good trim and was characterised as usual by a flexibility of which its owner took full advantage and rendered his parts with his fine organ under full control and with an amount of expression*

---

[47] 'The May Queen' *Herts Advertiser*, 9 December 1893

and feeling which imparted both life and soul to the music.

Miss Annie Kearton was soon discovered to be a young artiste of great talent apparently inheriting some of her parent's qualifications for charming a discriminating musical audience. She has insofar as it is possible for male and female vocal organs to assimilate a voice of the same purity and liquidity combined with the power of expressing every word with sweetness and clearness. Perhaps THE feature of her performance was the remarkable ease with which she uttered both the music of her part and the language that accompanied it. Her sister's voice was of lower range and was more of ordinary capacity, but her singing was allied with that excellent enunciation which is one of the characteristics of the family. Miss Helen Kearton played on the violin, was hardly suited with the piece as she played, and would no doubt have appeared to greater advantage with something more suitable to her youth - 10½ years [48]

Annie Kearton continued to sing with her father, sometimes alongside the Westminster Singers, until her marriage to Percy Runicles in 1896. Helen Kearton continued her violin studies, probably also until she got married, and was recorded in the 1901 Census, aged 18, as a professional violinist.

This leaves Caroline and Joseph's eldest son – Thomas Wilfred Coles Kearton. In the 1881 Census, the first since the family moved to London, Thomas Wilfred Coles Kearton was not with

---

[48] 'Mr Gale's Annual Concert' Andover Chronicle, 9 February 1894

them. Where was he? He was a boarding pupil at Thomas Cross's school in Bessborough Gardens, receiving a musical education. Known by his middle name, Wilfred, he was truly Joseph Harper Kearton's legacy, and his obituary in June 1937 deserves to be reproduced here in full:

We regret to record the death which took place at a Redhill nursing home in the early hours of yesterday (Thursday) morning of Mr. T Wilfred Kearton of Cockshot Road, Reigate. Mr. Kearton had undergone a serious illness by reason of which he was unable to avail himself of the important invitation extended to him recently to take part in the singing at the coronation service of King George VI at Westminster Abbey. He for some time was associated with Mr Godfrey Searle in the choral work at Saint Mary's, Reigate, and here his many friends have shown deep concern in his prolonged illness. He was a man of liberal musical attainment, having inherited from his father, founder of the Westminster Singers, a beautiful and powerful tenor voice.

His musical career was extraordinarily interesting. At the age of four, his treble voice displayed exceptional qualifications and he was immediately placed in the care of a good teacher and at the age of eight gained his first musical success in winning a choristership at St George's, Windsor, under the late Sir George Elvery. He became regarded as Queen Victoria's favourite solo boy. [...]

Outstanding Musical Career

At the age of 21, Mr. Kearton was re-appointed to the choir as principal tenor soloist and the following are a few of the outstanding functions he sang at:- Queen Victoria's Diamond Jubilee, the coronation of King Edward VII and King George V, and the funeral services of Queen Victoria and King Edward VII. A distinguished honour was also conferred upon Mr. Kearton. He received a royal command to give a recital of sacred and secular songs in the Royal Drawing Room at Windsor Castle. He was presented on that occasion to her late Majesty by the Master of the Queen's Musick, after which he and Sir Arthur Sullivan preceded with a programme of numbers selected from the latter's own compositions. Both were afterwards heartily congratulated by the Queen.

On his retirement from the royal choir Mr. Kearton was presented with an address, bound in vellum, from the residents of Windsor and Eton, inscribed "Many of your friends and a number of worshippers at St. George's Chapel, Windsor Castle, on hearing of your retirement from the choir after a period of service exceeding over 25 years feel they could not allow you to leave Windsor without some small token of their high appreciation of your beautiful singing, and which has always been a source of great delight to all who had the pleasure of hearing you." The album contains the names of signatories to the gift including Prince and Princess Christian of Schleswig-Holstein,

95

Earl Cadogan, Earl of Rosebery and Midlothian, the Duke of Wellington, the Earl of Durham, Lord Stamfordham, and the Dean of Windsor (the late Very Rev. P.F. Elliott.

A Special Mission

After leaving Windsor Mr. Kearton's services were soon taken up and Dr George Martin offered him St Paul's Cathedral and the tenor solo work at Saint Peters, Eton square. Subsequently he was selected by the British government for a special mission of musical propaganda in Scandinavia and Russia. Upon his father's death he succeeded him in the Westminster Singers remaining with that quartette for over 17 years. During his career he took part in prominent choral works at the Albert Hall and Queens Hall and in Gaiety Theatre operatic productions. He was also the chosen soloist at many of the big oratorio festivals including Liverpool, Three Choirs, Norwich, Hereford, Cheltenham etc. Locally, it is recalled, he was engaged for solo work at St. John's, Redhill, in the Choral Society's rendering of "Elijah", at Blechingley in "Hiawatha", and at the Central Hall, Redhill, in JH Maunder's "Hymn of Praise". He will be greatly missed at Saint Mary's, Reigate, where his fine solo work was always appreciated to the full, and his assistance in training the young choristers had highly valued response.

It is understood that the choristers will attend his funeral at St. Mary's on Saturday at 3:00 PM[49]

---

[49] 'Mr TW Kearton – death of a well-known Reigate vocalist' *Surrey Mirror*, 18 June 1937

Thomas Johnson (1805-1873)

At the age of 61, Thomas Johnson was one of the oldest of the men who participated in the Castle Yard riot. Despite this, he had a very young family, his youngest daughter Hannah being only four months old.

Eliza Perfect, the mother of this young family, was more than 20 years his junior, and was his second wife. He had married Eliza in 1856. No father's name was given for Thomas on their marriage certificate. Therefore, although there are several possible Thomas Johnsons in the parish registers born around 1805, the best fit is maybe the illegitimate son of Mary Johnson, baptised on 7 July 1805.

Newspaper reports of the riot, however, imply that Thomas was the brother of William Johnson, the footpath reformer. William's lineage is easier to reconstruct – his parents were William Johnson, a blacksmith, and Mary (formerly Waddington). If Mary was mother to both William and Thomas, she was already married to William Johnson the blacksmith when she had Thomas, so there is the question of why would he be recorded as illegitimate?

The family was living at Fisher's Gardens when little Hannah was born.

It is not clear what happened to Thomas after the riot, although he and Eliza had two more daughters after he was released from prison, baby Eliza being born in the summer of 1871. When the Census was taken in April 1871, Eliza and the family were at home in Wellington Street, Eliza was pregnant, and Thomas was "temporarily absent".

There is however a Thomas Johnson of the right age, married, and coming from Knaresborough, lodging at the Forester's Inn, Linton near Grassington. He was working as a linen weaver. The innkeeper, one Metcalfe Maxfield, was also a stone mason.

Thomas Johnson died in 1873. **After his widow Eliza died in 1880, Hannah, who was the tiny baby at the time of the riot and now 14, was taken in by George Renton's elderly grandfather and given a job.**

Henry Dixon (1804-1879)

Henry Dixon's occupation was given as Furniture broker, a job that the Censuses show he did for at least five years either side of his imprisonment. White's Directory (1866) places his business on Cheapside. He may however have at other times been a linen weaver like his father, John Dixon, before him. There is a Henry Dixon born Knaresborough, right age, *linen weaver*, visiting the Ellerbys at 10 Regent Street Leeds in the 1851 Census. Mary Ellerby is his sister Mary Dixon.

In 1861 and 1871 he is recorded as being married. There is, however, no sign of a wife, nor indeed a definitive marriage record. He was living alone in Gracechurch Street in 1861 and boarding with the Gamble family at Raw Gap in 1871.

Beyond this, Henry Dixon's life is something of a mystery.

He passed away in 1879.

William Ranson (1817-1890)

William Ranson was born in the winter of 1818 the eldest son of William Ranson senior, a sawyer, and his wife Sarah Dawe.

He was baptised on the 14th of January 1818. This may have been a rushed private affair which sometimes happened if a newborn was sickly and may not live as there was a second baptism some years later, on the 21st of February 1823, when he would have been "received into the church".

The family was often living on the edge of poverty. They rented their home in Briggate from William Duffield. For some of the time while their children were growing up, William's father enlisted in the navy so that Sarah would have some money to pay the rent and bring up the little ones. Nevertheless, it was not always enough; in 1841 William Ranson senior found himself in the borough debtors' prison. Eventually they appear to have got by on his Greenwich out-pension (the pension paid to retired seamen who did not need residential care in the Greenwich Hospital), until he died in 1856.

William junior was a young man in the winter of 1839, when he married the girl down the road, Ann Grayson in St John's Church. Ann was the daughter of Thomas Grayson, a labourer. Both families were living on Briggate. William had a trade. He was a shoemaker.

The newly-weds moved into a cottage in Windsor Lane, joined 18 months later by Ann's mother, now widowed, and brother James who worked at the linen mill. Their daughter Hannah came along within a year of their marriage.

By the time the next Census came around in 1851, the Ransons' little cottage on Windsor Lane was by far the most crowded household in the street. They had five little children, the youngest being a baby of 3 months. Ann's mother, aged 76, was receiving poor relief. And they had an elderly lodger, 81-year-old William Slinger, also a pauper.

Their children were much the same age as Joseph Kearton and may have known him from school.

William's wife Ann and his father died not long after each other. It is not clear what happened to the children immediately after their mother's death, but one assumes they spent some time in the workhouse and were forced to grow up fast.

That year, the County Borough Police Act 1856 came into force, leading to the establishment of the West Riding Constabulary, headquarters in Wakefield. 354 officers were recruited in the first year, amongst whom was William Ranson, Warrant No 263, sworn in on Christmas Eve. He no doubt looked fine in his uniform – five feet eight inches tall, with dark brown hair, grey eyes and a sallow complexion. On the 23rd January 1857 he was assigned to his division, on 13th April he was dismissed from the force for drunkenness!

Although he still considered himself a shoemaker (this is still given as his occupation in 1865 at the time of the Castle Yard riot) finding himself out of work again, he did what his father had done and worked as a wood sawyer.

A year later he married Widow Dinsdale, nee Margaret Bickerdike, nearly 20 years older than himself, at Ripon Cathedral. One feels there must have been more to this story, but I have not found it! Margaret moved into the cottage in Windsor Lane with him and his youngest son, Thomas aged 9.

Thus was the situation in 1865 when William and ten other men decided to take down Dr Simpson's fences, gates and fine shrubs that had encroached upon the public ground at Castle Yard. His children would have attended the school whose pupils had so offended Dr Simpson with their laughter. He was swept along by the rhetoric of the public meeting and encouraged by the beer supplied by young Renton. Before he knew it, he was arrested for riotous assembly.

Two years after the men's release from their three months in prison, Margaret Ranson died. William found himself living alone, rattling round the cottage in Windsor Lane that had once been the most crowded household in the street.

In 1873 he married for a third time, this time to widow Harriet Jennings nee Johnson. William got a new job, as a postman. They set up home at 2 Cistern Hill. Harriet's son Joseph moved in with them. When he was old enough to leave school, Joseph took an apprenticeship as a painter and continued living with them until his marriage to Isobel.

William Ranson passed away in 1890 at the age of 72.

Thomas Mawson (1812-1893)

Like William Ranson, at the time of the Castle Yard riot, 54-year-old Thomas Mawson and his wife Maria were living in the vicinity of Windsor Lane. Their cottage, in Calverley's Yard, was their home for the whole of their married life.

Even then the cottages were old. In 1876 a parcel of land that included 14 cottages and a weaving shed on Windsor Lane and Calverley's Yard were offered for sale. The 999-year lease had been granted in 1721.[50]

Thomas was a joiner and carpenter and was using the tools of his trade to saw off the bottom rail of the fence at the Castle Yard.

Thomas and Maria had been married for 33 years at the time of the riot but had no children. Thomas's younger brother, William Mawson, licensed victualler and innkeeper at the Black Swan was one of the men who prepared the dinner for the town celebrations on the 26th of June, and was married to Maria's sister Eliza Myers.

Thomas and William were the sons of William and Catharine Mawson, a Catholic family from Allerton Mauleverer. The family is listed in the Non-Parochial Registers, baby Thomas not then having received his name at his baptism and just listed as "Mawson".

After Maria's death in 1890, Thomas moved into the little two-roomed cottage at No.4 Bensons Yard on Briggate, which was to be his home until his own death three years later at the age of 81.

---

[50] 'Sales by Auction' *Knaresborough Post*, 22 April 1876

Peter Robinson (1845-1899)

On the day of the riot in 1865, Peter Robinson had been with two other youths, setting fire to Dr Simpson's summerhouse. He was a lad of 19, and still living at home at Powell's Yard behind Hilton Lane, with his family.

His father William Robinson was a journeyman[51] tailor, and his elder brother John William is recorded as a tailor's apprentice in the 1861 Census. It is likely that they knew the Johnsons (Thomas, one of the rioters, and his brother William Johnson the Footpath Reformer, who was a tailor by trade). Indeed, William Johnson may have at some point employed William Robinson as during the 1850s William and Jane Johnson lived just around the corner from the Robinsons on Beech Hill.

As well as Peter and John William, William and Sarah Robinson had three daughters – Emma (born circa 1841), Jane Ann (born circa 1847) and Eliza (born circa 1849). Powell's Yard remained the family home until Sarah died in 1872.

By the 1871 Census, all the Robinson children except Peter had moved on to new chapters in their lives. Emma was married and her 4-year-old daughter Eliza Jane was staying with her grandparents on the night of the census.

Peter himself followed suit not long after, marrying Ann Joplin at the Roman Catholic church of St Mary's in Knaresborough on the 4th of May 1871. Peter had been working as an iron moulder since he left school. He and Ann set up home in one of the little houses in Calcutt. Their first child, William, was born the

---

[51] A journeyman was a skilled craftsman who had usually learned their skills via an apprenticeship and was qualified as competent. Journeymen were employed by master craftsmen. Originally the term applied to people employed by the day (from the French word "journee") but it came to mean employed by any period.

following year. In all they had five children between 1872 and 1881.

However, by the time the 1891 Census came around, something had happened to break the family up. Ann now aged 50 was living with the children on Church Lane. Although still married to Peter, Ann is recorded as head of the household, and working as a grocer. The three eldest children all had jobs, and Jane and Joseph were still at school.

So where was Peter? Well, he can be found in the Census boarding at 14 Primitive Street, Leeds, with the family of Joseph Lee, a slotter and driller at the iron foundry. Peter Robinson was still employed as an iron moulder. One might think that he had been forced to travel to Leeds to find work. However, a search through the newspapers tells a different story. On the 21st of April 1886, at Knaresborough Petty Sessions, Mr Bateson, solicitor, presented an application from Ann Robinson for a judicial separation from her husband [52] . He had been convicted the previous week of beating and assaulting her. The application was granted, and Peter Robinson was ordered to pay 12s a week of the 25s a week that he earned as an iron moulder for the maintenance of Ann and their children.

He never returned to Knaresborough to live.

He died in the summer of 1899 aged 57 and is buried in Holbeck cemetery in Leeds.

Ann and the children remained in Knaresborough. She is listed as head of the household in their home in Church Lane where she was a self-employed grocer and dealer in provisions. Her daughter Jane lived with her until her death in 1903; Ann herself survived, living on her Old Age Pension, until 1919.

---

[52] 'Application for Judicial Separation' *Knaresborough Post*, Saturday 24 April 1886

The Judge – Mr Justice Shee

At the time of the Castle Yard trial, Mr Justice Shee was at the pinnacle of his career. He had become a judge of the Court of Queen's Bench less than two years previously – the first Roman Catholic judge since the reformation – at the same time receiving his knighthood to become Sir William Shee.

The Northern Circuit was his first after his elevation to the Bench and as such, when he passed sentence on the Knaresborough Eleven, he probably was still trying to prove a measure of firmness in his dealings as a Judge.

Career

William Shee was an Anglo-Irish politician, lawyer and judge. He was the son of Joseph Shee, an Irish gentleman from Kilkenny who had settled in South Lambeth to become a London merchant "of high repute and opulence". His mother Teresa Darell came from an old Catholic family of Kent.

Educated at the Roman Catholic College of St Cuthbert, Ushaw, Durham, and Edinburgh University, he was called to the Bar in 1828 and quickly rose to leader of the Home circuit.

As a barrister he was made serjeant-at-law in 1840 and appointed queen's serjeant in 1857. One of his most famous cases was the unsuccessful defence of the poisoner William Palmer, an English doctor found guilty of murder in one of the most notorious cases of the 19th century.

William Shee was a supporter of Catholic emancipation (a subject on which Dr John Simpson also expressed views as a young man) and failed in an attempt to contest the parliamentary seat for Marylebone in 1847. He did however succeed in the 1852 general election, standing for Kilkenny County. As an MP he became active in Irish Tenants' rights, but does not appear to have succeeded in any of his actions, and failed to be re-elected in 1857 and 1859.

After the trial of the Knaresborough Eleven

Less than two years after the Castle Yard trial William Shee died – according to his obituary in the York Herald, of "some affection of the throat"[53]. According to his biography in the *Oxford Dictionary of National Biography,* however, he died at home in London of apoplexy (an old word for stroke)[54]

[53] 'Obituary of Sir William Shee', *York Herald*, 22 Feb 1868

[54] Barker, G. F. R. (2004) "*Shee, Sir William (1804–1868)*", rev. Hugh Mooney, Oxford Dictionary of National Biography, Oxford University Press

The complainant - Dr John Simpson

At the time of the riot in 1865, Dr John Simpson was aged 72, a physician "not practicing", and a magistrate of the West Riding. He had been married for nearly 40 years and was living the life of a gentleman, primarily at 21 Gloucester Place, in Portman Square, Marylebone, but Castle Lodge was his country residence and arguably where his heart was.

The aspirations of young John Simpson, MD

Forty years earlier as a young man, recently qualified from Edinburgh University, he had worked in Bradford at the behest of his benefactor, his uncle Dr John Simpson of Malton. He briefly kept a journal in 1825. This provides an interesting insight into his aspirations and a glimpse of the man he would become.

It is interesting to read his opinion about keeping traditional customs alive, as this view seems to have deserted him later when he annexed the traditional recreation area of the people of Knaresborough within his Castle Lodge pleasure grounds.

> *"I am jealous as a man can be of the liberty of the subject, but can see nothing, in keeping up, and strictly observing the old customs and national sports of the country, that militates against the liberty of the subject. On the contrary it keeps up a national spirit and feeling amongst us. It reminds us that we are a peculiar people, that we are Englishmen. And so long as we are sensible of that, and retain the spirit of those ancestors who have handed down to us those very sports, we may laugh at all the efforts of our enemies, whether foreign or domestic. Those old customs are kept up more at Knaresborough*

than any other place I know. Here there is the old Saxon or Danish sword dance kept up, also Guisers, Mummers, Plough Stotts and a whole catalogue of Christmas festivities, and I hope never to see them abolished and forgot."

Dr John Simpson, Bradford, 1825

Family

Two years after leaving Bradford, John Simpson married Elizabeth Ward, daughter of Thomas and Eleanor Ward, in her home parish of Handsworth near Sheffield. The ceremony was performed by her uncle the Rev. Andrew Hudleston, Eleanor's brother.

Elizabeth came from a long line of Rev. Hudlestons on her mother's side going back to at least the 1600s in Cumberland.

Their first child, named Wilfred Hudleston Simpson, was born on 2 June 1828, and baptised the same day. He was more formally baptised in Handsworth on 8 May 1829.

They went on to have four more children – Eleanor Blanche (b.1829), Agnes Anne (b.1831), John Henry (b.1834), and Rosa Elizabeth (b.1835)

Cayton Hall

Their youngest child, Rosa, was born at Cayton, South Stainley (and baptised the same day as Sarah, the daughter of the household's coachman James Stabler). The family had rented Low Cayton Grange (later known as Cayton Hall) from Charles Standish around 1834. The house and farm were not in a good state of repair and for three years Dr Simpson claimed a rent rebate on account of a leaky roof and fields that drained badly. Nevertheless, at Cayton, John Simpson was finally living the life for which he had yearned, a grand home in the country with nine servants freeing him up to follow his rural pursuits.

In 1842 the tenancy of Low Cayton Grange passed to friend and magistrate Thomas Clifton Wilkinson and his family, and the Simpsons moved to their London residence in Marylebone. Cayton Hall eventually returned to the latest in the long line of Rev. Hudlestons – John and Elizabeth's son John Henry.

Meanwhile it seems his house in Knaresborough for a while stood empty. In the 1840s he let some of the land around it in three plots as gardens.

Castle Lodge

It wasn't until the family had moved to their London home (21 Gloucester Place in Portland Square, Marylebone) in the 1850s, that John Simpson started to show an interest in his country residence at Castle Lodge again. Spending more time there, he took back the land that had been let as gardens and additional land which he rented from Sir Charles Slingsby and from the Duke of Devonshire and started developing the pleasure grounds of his dreams. Some of the expensive trees and shrubs that he had planted were said to have had 15-20 years growth by the time of the riot[55].

Agnes and Rosa Simpson, described as the 2nd and 3rd daughters of Dr John Simpson, MD, were recorded as living there in the Census immediately before the Castle Yard affair, together with their gardener, cook and housemaid. Edwin Smith, clerk to the Improvement Commissioners, lived next door at Castle Cliff for many years. Thomas Benson, whitesmith and bell hanger, who claimed that he had heard John Winterburn threaten to chop the gardener's legs off, was living on Kirkgate near the entrance to Dr Simpson's Yard.

---

[55] Castle Yard Trial report

Simpson had begun to put up boundaries around his grounds – wooden fences, iron palisades, stone pillars and iron gates, some parts of which encroached on the land which the people of the town used for recreation and the main footpath down to the waterside. Almost immediately the townspeople responded by breaking down the gates. The ensuing legal action found in favour of the gate-breakers and he had been forced on more than one occasion to move his boundaries back several yards.

After the trial

About a year after the trial, Dr John Simpson and all his family changed their surname by Royal Licence to Hudleston.

Six months after that he died, and as "John Hudleston formerly Simpson, of London, aged 74" his death was registered in Marylebone. His estate was valued at "under £25000" (worth around £1,956,930 in 2022). The remaining family continued to live at Gloucester Place until his wife's death in 1878.

John Hudleston, formerly Simpson, was buried at Rillington near Malton, where he owned around 400 acres of land, inherited from the uncle who had put him through university.

Part IV: The legacy of the tankards

This story may have been lost forever were it not for the legacy of the tankards. Several generations after the event, the tankards started turning up for descendants to find amongst the possessions of their relatives who had passed. The inscriptions aroused curiosity and questions were asked.

It might be said that, in doing so, they fulfilled their destiny.

When the tankards were presented to the men, the chairman of the reception committee said,

> *"The cups were not only a testimonial of the sympathy of their fellow townsman but also a certificate which they could at all times produce with pride and pleasure, if at any future time anyone should be base and mean enough to taunt them with having been imprisoned. If ever they found themselves in that position, there they would have a testimony to produce that what they had done had been for the good of the ancient town, and what they had suffered, they had suffered for the freedom of their fellow townsman."[56]*

In the longer term the tankards were a focus to ensure that the story of the Castle Yard would never be forgotten.

---

[56] 'Return home of the Knaresborough rioters' The Knaresborough Post, Saturday, June 30th, 1866

"May each and every one hand it down untarnished and unsullied for future generations"[57]

Twelve tankards were commissioned – one for each of the rioters, and the twelfth was for William Johnson, the footpath reformer. Supplied by Mr TF Gibson, ironmonger of Knaresborough, they were made of embossed and hallmarked silver plate and described as "exceedingly pretty".

In 2014, Thomas Johnson's great-grandson, Howard S. Johnson, whose ancestor's cup is still with his family today, was prompted to ask what they knew of its history. On discovering that the men had been urged to pass the tankards down through the generations to ensure the story would not be forgotten, he set about trying to find the rest of the tankards and try and return them to their families. A photograph of his great-grandfather's tankard can be seen in Howard's blog.[58]

He discovered that descendants of several other of the rioters had also been inspired to research the events of 1865-6, and at least two others of the tankards are still with their recipients' families today.

Joseph Kearton's tankard is now in Ireland. Its present owner says,

> *"Years ago, my grandfather worked as a plumber in Knaresborough, he did some work for a couple of ladies who lived next door to him and they gave him the tankard as payment. Apparently, he knew very little about it but eventually gave it to my father*

---

[57] 'Reception of the Knaresbro rioters' Ripon and Richmond Chronicle, Saturday, June 30th, 1866
[58] *Do you know about the Knaresborough Riot?*, Howard S Johnson, https://knaresboroughriot.wordpress.com/

who treasured it, he was so proud of his Knaresborough roots and absolutely loved local history. "

William Ranson's tankard turned up at an auction in Scarborough a few years ago and was bought with a view to returning to its legitimate family should a descendant be found. Strangely the inscription is missing from the crest, the writing simply saying William Ranson, Knaresborough, 26 June 1866.

Maybe you know the whereabouts of another of the tankards, or can add to the story. If so, Knaresborough Town Museum would be delighted to hear from you.

Email: info@knaresboroughtownmuseum.org

Verse: The Trial of the Knaresborough Eleven

The Judge Shee sat in her robes of state.
"The Eleven" they waited to hear their fate,
The Counsel, he stated the case aloud
To the Judge, the Jury and the listening crowd;

He said how on one fine October day
"The Eleven" asserted their right to play
On a piece of ground on the Castle hill
Of a town where the ladies are famed for skill.

He said, how a Doctor who lived hard by
On that same piece of ground had cast his eye,
And thinking he'd like it his garden to be
Had fenced it around – and he bow'd to Judge Shee.

He said, how the boys, the land to retrieve,
Had begun their game without asking leave;
How the balls had uprooted both tree and flower
And set on fire the Doctor's bower;

He said how the Doctor with rage inflamed
Had summoned for riot the eleven he named;

'Twixt babes at school and boys at play,
He had no peace for many a day.
(for the National school was near the ground
And children will sometimes laugh out loud).

So now in despair he made a stand
And sued for peace to the law of the land.

The Judge Shee listened, the Judge Shee heard
Her heart was the Doctor's at every word;
No need for the Counsel to say much more,
The Judge Shee had pleaded his cause before.

"The Eleven" their counsel now strove to defend,
And many a townsman stood forth their friend.
They proved they had a right to play on the
ground.
The Doctor's right – it could not be found,

For the public they'd taken the matter in hand,
And without a riot they reclaimed the land.
There were ladies he said, who watched without
fear;
Policemen and constables they too were near;

Two magistrates also were on the ground,
But said not one word to disperse the crowd;
Tho' had they thought fit to forbid the game
The lads would have quietly gone as they came.

The Judge Shee no dignified silence would keep
Till both sides were heard in a matter so deep,
But questioned and argued to get her own way
And strove by her own will the jury to sway;

* And decided that a tumult, though only of three,*
Is a riot henceforth by the law of Judge Shee,
Provided that only one person will say
That a lad used a threat tho' 'twas only in play.

If he was not afraid why it will surely be seen
That he might, could, would, should, ought to have
been.

The jury they thought the Judge Shee knew best,
And yielded the verdict to her behest.

The foreman said "guilty", but as we don't see it
We hope in your sentence you mix mercy wi'it.

The Judge Shee was glad she could mercy bestow,
And as they'd not trespassed or hurt any foe,
She would give them three months and then let
them go.

So I lift up my voice and cry out – So ho!
That is mercy and judgement together I trow.
If ever I'm tried, oh not by Judge Shee!
I hope that the Shee Judge will never judge me.

This piece of satirical verse was freely circulating at the town celebrations on the release of the men and printed in the *Richmond and Ripon Chronicle*, 30th June 1866

List of characters

ACKRILL, Robert – reporter, witness at Thomas Benson's perjury hearing

ARCHY, Gilbert – police sergeant, witness at the trial of the Eleven

BARKER, Thomas – rioter

BENSON, Thomas – Dr Simpson's neighbour, last minute witness at the trial of the Eleven, subsequently accused of perjury

BLACKBURN, Mr – barrister for the defence at the initial hearing and the trial

BROOKS, Fleming – police officer at the riot

BURGESS, William – Dr Simpson's gardener, key witness at the trial of the Eleven and at Thomas Benson's perjury hearing

CAMPBELL FOSTER, Mr – barrister for the prosecution at the trial

DIGBY SEYMOUR QC, Mr - barrister for the defence at the trial

DIXON, Henry - rioter

EASTBROOK, - police officer at the riot

FLACKLEY, James – witness at Thomas Benson's perjury hearing

FLETCHER, James – rioter

GILL, Matthew – solicitor's clerk

HARESS, William – witness at Thomas Benson's perjury hearing

HUDSON, William Barret – police officer at the riot

JOHNSON, Thomas – rioter

JOHNSON, William – footpath reform activist, brother of rioter Thomas Johnson

KEARTON, Joseph (Harper) – rioter

MAWSON, Thomas – rioter

MAWSON, William – publican, brother of rioter Thomas Mawson

MIDDLETON, Mr – barrister for the prosecution at the initial hearing and the trial, and counsel for the defence for Thomas Benson at his perjury hearing

MYERS, Edward – publican, brother-in-law of rioter Thomas Mawson

ORMSBY, Robert – police inspector, witness at the trial of the Eleven and at Thomas Benson's perjury hearing

PROCTER, William – rioter

RANSON, William – rioter

RENTON, George junior – rioter

RENTON, George senior – grandfather of George Renton junior and Sheriff's Officer

ROBINSON, Peter – rioter

SHAW, Mr – counsel for the prosecution at Thomas Benson's perjury hearing

SHEE, Sir William – Justice at the trial of the Eleven

SHEPHERD, Mr – defence counsel for George Renton at the trial

SIMPSON, John, M.D. – the complainant, owner of Castle Lodge

SNOWDEN, John – witness at Thomas Benson's perjury hearing

WINTERBURN MASON, John ("Jack") – rioter

Bibliography

The **newspaper coverage** of the riot story took place over a period of six months. It first came to people's attention after the eleven men were summoned to appear at an initial hearing in Knaresborough courthouse on Wednesday 1st November and Friday 3rd November 1865. Newspapers throughout the region told and re-told the events of October 3rd from different perspectives following the trial itself, the perjury hearing of Thomas Benson, and ultimately the celebrations on the men's release in June 1866. I have listed the most significant of the reports below.

All the newspapers listed in this bibliography are available to view and download on Find My Past (by subscription) and the British Newspaper Archive (by subscription or pay as you go). Quotations are reproduced from my own transcriptions of the newspaper text with kind permission of the British Newspaper Archive and are copyright-free. Unsigned newspaper text goes out of copyright 70 calendar years after the year of publication, and signed newspaper text goes out of copyright 70 calendar years after the death of the author(s).

Although the local newspaper, the *Knaresborough Post*, published today by Johnstone Press plc, was founded as early as 1863, at the time of writing the earliest issue that has been digitised and made available in the British Newspaper Archive online is from 1868 – too late for coverage of the riot. Amazingly however, the story of the town's celebrations, which was covered in considerable detail in the Knaresborough Post on 30th June 1866, was written out longhand in the 1925 school exercise book of one Sidney Horner of Knaresborough and has been transcribed in full in *For the Old Age Perishers of Knaresborough 1994* listed below.

The Initial Hearing

'Dr Simpson and the Vicar of Knaresbro' – Castle Yard Riots [from our own reporter]', *Richmond and Ripon Chronicle*, Saturday 4th November 1865

'The Castle Yard riot' *Bradford Observer*, 9th November 1865

'The recent destruction of Dr Simpson's pleasure grounds *Yorkshire Gazette*, 4th November 1865

The Trial

'The Knaresborough Riot question of public right' *Sheffield Daily Telegraph*, 7th April 1866

'The Knaresborough Rioters' *Leeds Intelligencer*, 7th April 1866

'The Knaresborough Riot' *Leeds Intelligencer*, 14th April 1866 – letter to the Home Secretary

'Riot at Knaresborough' *York Herald*, 14 April 1866

The Perjury Hearing

'The Late Knaresborough Riot' *Richmond and Ripon Chronicle*, 12th May 1866 – detailed account, including verbatim witness statements

'The Knaresborough Riot charge of perjury' *Leeds Intelligencer*, 12th May 1866

'The Knaresborough Riot' *Leeds Intelligencer*, 19th May 1866 – John Simpson's letter to the Editor

The Celebrations

Mountain, John, *For the Old Age Perishers of Knaresborough 1994*, (1995), available in the reference section of Knaresborough library

'Reception of the Knaresboro Rioters - grand demonstration'
Richmond and Ripon Chronicle, 30th June 1866

The previous incidents

'The Battle of Knaresborough' *Leeds Intelligencer,* 26th April 1862

'The disputed footway in the Castle Yard' *Leeds Mercury*, 22nd April 1862

Bradford Observer, 18 May 1854 - Sir Charles Slingsby dropped dozens of writs against Messrs Johnson and co regarding enclosure of the Flatt

Yorkshire, England, Quarter Session records, 1634-1914, *Ancestry.com* - 19 July 1860, Wakefield Session, indictment for riot

The characters

Baptism, marriage and burial records for all eleven rioters and their families, and Dr John Simpson, have been traced using a combination of Ancestry, Find My Past (which has digital images of many of the parish records) and The Genealogist.

Census records, taken at 10-yearly intervals from 1841 to 1911, show where the person was living (and sometimes how many rooms), their occupation, and their year of birth. Digital images of most of these have been viewed on Ancestry.

Wherever possible, evidence from several different sources has been cross-referenced to verify that we have the correct person.

In some instances there is additional information from land records, directories and electoral rolls.

Richer details of the lives of three of the men – John Winterburn, George Renton and Joseph Kearton – have been found using newspapers from the British Newspaper Archive.

James Fletcher

Baptism of James Fletcher, 19 June 1814
Baptism of Jane Thompson, 21 October 1814
Baptism of Mary Thompson, 28 May 1813
Marriage to Jane Thompson, Q1 1856
Burial of James Fletcher, 29 April 1866
1851 Census
1861 Census
1871 Census for Jane Fletcher
1881 Census for Jane Fletcher

'Death of one of the Knaresborough rioters' *Leeds Intelligencer*, 28th April 1866

Thomas Barker

Baptism, 7 January 1844
Death index (Q2 1866)
Death certificate, 30 June 1866
Probate, 4 August 1877
1851 Census
1861 Census

John Winterburn Mason

Birth certificate, born 13 Mar 1848 West End, Fewston, mother Mary Mason formerly Winterburn, no father given
Baptism, 29 March 1848, John Winterburn, illegitimate son of Mary Mason, widow
Marriage to Grace Barrick, May 16 1869, John Winterburn Mason whitesmith, no father given, Grace's father Joseph Barrick weaver
Marriage to Emily Herring, 25 December 1877, John's father given as John Mason
Electoral register (1918), living on Waterside
Death, Q2 1919
1851 Census

1861 Census
1871 Census
1881 Census
1891 Census
1901 Census
1911 Census

John Winterburn Mason's active role in the town on behalf of the Knaresborough working man was documented in the Knaresborough Post newspaper throughout his life. There are numerous references to his activities in the Star Angling Club, the Gas and Waterworks Committee of the Urban District Council, and the Knaresborough Floral Horticultural and Fanciers Show. The following are just a selection of the references.

'Knaresbro Star Angling Club' *Knaresborough Post*, 13 November 1880

'Knaresbro Star Angling Club' *Knaresborough Post*, 9 November 1889, on the occasion of their 15th anniversary supper

'Knaresborough Star Angling Association' *Knaresborough Post*, 14 November 1896

'Knaresborough Star Angling Association' *Knaresborough Post*, 16 November 1912

'Alarming fire at Knaresbro' *Knaresborough Post*, 24 June 1882

'Knaresborough Floral Horticultural and Fanciers Show' *Knaresborough Post*, 1 September 1888

'NER Ambulance Class' *Knaresborough Post,* 18 December 1897

'Letter to the Editor' *Knaresborough Post*, 27 April 1895

'Gas and Water Committee' *Knaresborough Post,* 13 June 1896

'Gas and Water Committee' *Knaresborough Post,* 8 May 1897

George Renton

Baptism, 15 January 1845
1851 Census
1861 Census
1871 Census
1881 Census
1891 Census
1901 Census
1911 Census
1841 Census for George Renton, Snr.
1851 Census for George Renton, Snr.
1881 Census for George Renton, Snr.
Marriage to Rose Bertha Shutt, 28 November 1878, St Peter's, Harrogate
Gravestone Photograph Index, 1265-2014 – burial 1923
England & Wales, National Probate Calendar (Index of Wills and Administrations), 1858-1995 – death given as 21 November 1923, probate granted 12 Jan 1924

There are many advertisements in the Knaresborough Post for auctions undertaken by Renton and Renton. In addition, the same newspaper covers meetings of the Improvement Commissioners, election of overseers etc. which reference both George Renton junior and senior, some of which are listed below.

'Election of Commissioners' *Knaresborough Post*, 9 May 1874

'Overseers of the Claro Division' *Knaresborough Post*, 1 April 1876

'Knaresbro Improvement Commissioners' *Knaresborough Post*, 6 May 1876

Joseph Harper Kearton

The references below relate specifically to Joseph Harper Kearton. I have however also investigated the records for his parents, wife and children.

Birth
Baptism, 12 November 1848
Marriage, 10 January 1870, St Cuthberts, Wells
Burial, 10 February 1914, St Michael and All Angels, Southwick
Probate, 16 May 1914, granted to Caroline Kearton
Death certificate
1841 Census for George Kearton and Ann Harper, in service for the Rev.T Collins
1851 Census
1861 Census
1871 Census
1881 Census
1891 Census
1901 Census
1911 Census
1911 Census for Caroline Kearton
Lunacy Patients Admissions Register (1912), Joseph Harper Kearton admitted 13 Mar 1912 to West Sussex Asylum, discharged 28 Feb 1913, recovered
School admission (1881) for Thomas Wifred Coles Kearton, born 17 Jul 1871

Dix, R. CowGill, C. Bashford, S. McVeigh and R. Ridgewell (2014-). *British Musical Biography* online. (online version of J. Brown and S. Stratton, 1897). InConcert Project. accessed 20 Jul 2022. http://datatodata.com/in-concert/BMB/

Rev. RV Taylor BA. "Yorkshire Musicians", *The Knaresborough Post*, 10 November 1888, p4, https://search.findmypast.co.uk/bna/viewarticle?id=bl%2f00020 31%2f18881110%2f051&stringtohighlight=j%20harper

"Obituary: J. Harper Kearton." *The Musical Times*, vol. 55, no. 853, 1914, pp. 178–178. JSTOR, http://www.jstor.org/stable/906279 – includes a photo of Kearton by Arthur Weston

Queen Victoria's Golden Jubilee performance of Te Deum https://en.wikipedia.org/wiki/Golden_Jubilee_of_Queen_Victor ia

Holloway Sanatorium https://en.wikipedia.org/wiki/Holloway_Sanatorium

Searches for J Harper Kearton and the Westminster Singers in the British Newspaper Archive yield more than 450 results. These are just a selection:

'The "Messiah" at Knaresbro' *Knaresborough Post,* 22 December 1877

'From the provinces – Bristol' *The Lute*, 1 Jun 1886

Rev. RV Taylor BA. "Yorkshire Musicians", *The Knaresborough Post*, 10 November 1888, p4

'The Cardiff popular concerts' *South Wales Daily News*, 28 November 1892

'Mr GM Fermor's Concert' *Middlesex Independent*, 18 November 1893

'Mr Gale's Annual Concert' *Andover Chronicle*, 9 February 1894

'Westminster Glee Singers and Royal Artillery Band concert' *Dover Express,* 29 August 1909

Mr TW Kearton – death of a well-known Reigate vocalist' Surrey Mirror, 18 June 1937

William Procter

Baptism of William Procter, 16 June 1809
Marriage to Jane Appleton, 17 June 1833
Marriage to Mary Fairburn, 2 August 1856
Marriage of James Procter to Mary Fairburn, 20 Dec 1855
1841 Census
1851 Census
1861 Census
1881 Census
Burial of Mary Procter, 2 May 1866
Death certificate for Mary Procter

'Deaths' *Knaresborough Post*, 12th March 1887 – William Procter obituary

Thomas Johnson

Baptism of Thomas "son of Mary Johnson Illegit.", 7 July 1805
Marriage to Sarah Thorp, 27 August 1827
Burial of Sarah Johnson, 30 December 1855
Marriage to Eliza Perfect, 20 July 1856
Burial, 28 October 1873
1841 Census
1851 Census
1861 Census
1871 Census

William Johnson, the footpath reformer

Baptism, 7 July 1805
Death, Q2 1872
1841 Census
1851 Census
1861 Census
1871 Census

Henry Dixon

Baptism, 6 May 1804
1851 Census
1861 Census
1871 Census
Death, Q1 1879
1866 White's Directory,
https://specialcollections.le.ac.uk/digital/collection/p16445coll4/id/68685/rec/2

William Ranson

Baptism, 14 January 1818
Baptism, 27 February 1823
Marriage to Ann Grayson, 3 February 1839
Marriage to Margaret Bickerdike, 14 October 1858
Marriage to Harriet Jennings, 1873
Death, Q2 1890
1841 Census
1851 Census
1861 Census
1871 Census
1881 Census

West Riding Constabulary, Examination Book A, 1856-1857.
West Yorkshire, England, Police Records, 1833-1919

Thomas Mawson

Baptism, 14 January 1812 at St Mary's Catholic church in
Allerton Mauleverer
Marriage of Thomas Mawson to Maria Myers, 11 September
1832
Marriage of William Mawson to Eliza Myers, Q4 1843
Death, Q3 1893
1841 Census

1851 Census
1861 Census
1871 Census
1881 Census
1891 Census

Peter Robinson

Baptism, 27 July 1845
Marriage to Ann Joplin, 4 May 1871
1851 Census
1861 Census
1871 Census
1881 Census
1891 Census
'Application for Judicial Separation' *Knaresborough Post*,
Saturday 24 April 1886
Death given as 21 Jun 1899 on
https://www.findagrave.com/memorial/226544050/peter-robinson

Dr John Simpson

Baptism, 17 May 1793
Marriage to Elizabeth Ward, 22 August 1827, Handsworth,
York
1841 Census
1851 Census
1861 Census
Death Q4 1867
England & Wales, National Probate Calendar (Index of Wills
and Administrations), 1858-1995 – death given as 8 October
1867, probate granted 5 December 1867

The Journal of Dr John Simpson of Bradford 1825, City of Bradford Metropolitan Council, Libraries Division – Local Studies Department, 1881 ISBN 0 907734 00 6

Stainley and Cayton, Hudleston, N.A., G.A. Pindar and Son Ltd (1956)

Mr Justice Shee

Marriage to Mary Gordon of Banffshire, 26 Dec 1837
1851 Census
Death Q1 1868
England & Wales, National Probate Calendar (Index of Wills and Administrations), 1858-1995 – death given as 19 February 1868, probate granted 14 March 1868

'Death of Mr Justice Shee' *The York Herald*, 22 February 1868

'Sir William Shee - the Queen's Sergeant', *Old Kilkenny Review*, Kilkenny Archaeological Society

'Mr Justice Shee' *Illustrated London News,* 29 February 1868

There is an image of the Hon. William Shee, originally published in *Illustrated London News* (1864) reprinted in Knott (1912) "The Trial of William Palmer", on Wikipedia. It can be accessed at https://en.m.wikipedia.org/wiki/William_Shee

Maps

The maps in this book are reproduced (and in some cases annotated) with the permission of the National Library of Scotland, under the terms of the Creative Commons Attribution (CC-BY) licence.

They can be accessed at
https://maps.nls.uk/geo/explore/#zoom=15.0&lat=54.01036&lon=-1.46234&layers=117746212&b=1

They include:

SCRIVEN Ordnance Survey, Town Plans of England and Wales. Knaresborough Sheet 1, Surveyed: 1849, Published: 1851

BOND END Ordnance Survey, Town Plans of England and Wales. Knaresborough Sheet 2, Surveyed: 1849, Published: 1851

UNION WORKHOUSE Ordnance Survey, Town Plans of England and Wales. Knaresborough Sheet 3, Surveyed: 1849, Published: 1851

CASTLE YARD, HILTON LANE, HIGH STREET, BRIGGATE Ordnance Survey, Town Plans of England and Wales. Knaresborough Sheet 4, Surveyed: 1849, Published: 1851

WINDSOR LANE, YORK PLACE Ordnance Survey, Town Plans of England and Wales. Knaresborough Sheet 5, Surveyed: 1849, Published: 1851

LOW BRIDGE, SPITALCROFT, UNION INN Ordnance Survey, Town Plans of England and Wales. Knaresborough Sheet 6, Surveyed: 1849, Published: 1849

Cover print

Antique Lithograph - "Ruins of the Castle." by S Howell
published 1836 by Geo. Wilson, Knaresboro'.

9 781916 696082